Step **Forward** Language for Everyday Life

Workbook

SERIES DIRECTOR
Jayme Adelson-Goldstein

Introductory Level

Vanessa Caceres

OXFORD
UNIVERSITY PRESS

OXFORD
UNIVERSITY PRESS

198 Madison Avenue
New York, NY 10016 USA

Great Clarendon Street, Oxford OX2 6DP UK

Oxford University Press is a department of the University of Oxford.
It furthers the University's objective of excellence in research, scholarship,
and education by publishing worldwide in

Oxford New York

Auckland Cape Town Dar es Salaam Hong Kong Karachi
Kuala Lumpur Madrid Melbourne Mexico City Nairobi
New Delhi Shanghai Taipei Toronto

With offices in

Argentina Austria Brazil Chile Czech Republic France Greece
Guatemala Hungary Italy Japan Poland Portugal Singapore
South Korea Switzerland Thailand Turkey Ukraine Vietnam

OXFORD and OXFORD ENGLISH are registered trademarks of
Oxford University Press

© Oxford University Press 2008

Database right Oxford University Press (maker)

Editorial Director: Sally Yagan
Senior Publishing Manager: Stephanie Karras
Head of Project and Development Editors: Karen Horton
Managing Editor: Sharon Sargent
Associate Project Editor: Meredith Stoll
Design Director: Robert Carangelo
Design Project Manager: Maj-Britt Hagsted
Project Manager: Allison Harm
Production Manager: Shanta Persaud
Production Controller: Eve Wong
Packager: Bill Smith Studio

ISBN 978 0 19 4398442

Printed in China

20 19 18

Illustrations: Argosy Publishing: 14, 30, 62Shawn Banner: 73 Niki Barolini:
8, 10, 21, 23, 25, 28, 29, 35, 41, 42, 51, 56, 63, 64, 70, 76, 78 Barbara
Bastian: 3, 77, 81, 84 Kenneth Batelman: 65 John Batten: 12, 17, 18, 39,
45, 62, 79 Richard Carbajal/illustrationonline.com: 21, 31, 44, 67 Laurie
A. Conley: 24, 34, 50, 66 Bill Dickson/Contactjupiter.com: 13, 33 Jody
Emery: 48, 69, 72, 75 Mark Hannon: 2, 32, 46, 59, 68, 82 Kev Hopgood: 5,
33, 38, 48, 57, 61, 81 Rose Lowry: 4, 26, 52, 80 Mark Mones/AAReps.Inc.:
11, 20, 27, 32, 49, 55, 71 Pamorama.com: 6, 16, 51, 60, 74 Geo Parkin: 15,
37Roger Penwill: 30 Linda Pierce: 4, 41, 53, 83 Susan Spellman: 34, 40, 47,
55, 76 Simon Williams/illustrationweb.com.

Photographs: Susan Alexander/iStockphoto: 36 (coins); Burke/Triolo/
Jupiter Images: 36 (shoes); Gloria H. Chomica/Masterfile: 77 (room for
rent); D Berry/PhotoLink/age fotostock: 77 (house); D. Hurst/Alamy: 36
(socks); Dennis Kitchen Studio: 58; iStockPhoto: 36 (price tag); © Doring
Kindersley, 36 (pants); John Lund/Heather Hryciw/Getty Images: 24;
Steven S. Miric/SuperStock: 77 (apartment); Thomas Northcut/Getty
Images: 36 (sweater, shirt); Owen Price/iStockphoto: 77 (duplex); www.
photospin.com © 2007: 36 (dime, quarter)

Thanks to Elaine Langlois for her graceful editing and
Sharon Sargent for her editorial guidance. I enjoyed
working with everyone on the Oxford team.

I'm also grateful to my family and friends for their
patience as I worked early, early morning hours.

I thank my students for all of their inspiration and
support.

Vanessa Caeres

I gratefully acknowledge the contributions of the Intro
Workbook team. Thanks to author Vanessa Caceres
for engaging in higher-level thinking about low-level
exercises; development editor Elaine Langlois for asking
the right questions, production editors Meredith Stoll
and Katya Reno for their speed and accuracy; and Sharon
Sargent for being, well, Sharon.

Jayme Adelson-Goldstein

CONTENTS

Nice to Meet You

LESSON 1 Vocabulary

A Match the words with the pictures.

__1__ open	____ say	____ sign
____ close	____ check	____ circle

B Look at the pictures in A. Complete the sentences. Use the words in the box.

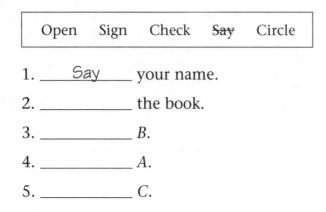

Open   Sign   Check   ~~Say~~   Circle

1. _____Say_____ your name.

2. _____ the book.

3. _____ *B*.

4. _____ *A*.

5. _____ *C*.

LESSON 2 **Life stories**

A Look at the picture. Complete the sentences. Use the words in the box.

| ~~first name~~   last name   middle name   signature |

Milford Adult School

Student ID

Lorena Carla Ortiz

ID 473968

Teacher: Rob Boatman

Lorena Carla Ortiz

1. My _____first name_____ is Lorena.

2. My _____ is Carla.

3. My _____ is Ortiz.

4. My _____ is *Lorena Carla Ortiz.*

B Look at the picture in A. Circle *yes* or *no*.

1. Rob Boatman is a student.   yes   (no)
2. I am a teacher.   yes   no
3. My last name is Ortiz.   yes   no
4. My first name is Carla.   yes   no
5. My ID number is 473968.   yes   no
6. My middle name is Lorena.   yes   no
7. I go to Adams Adult School.   yes   no
8. I am a student.   yes   no

A Look at the pictures. Write the words. Use *he, she, it,* or *they*.

1. ___they___   2. _____   3. _____

4. _____   5. _____   6. _____

B Complete the sentences. Circle *a* or *b*.

1. ____ is a man.

 a. She   b. He

2. ____ are students.

 a. He   b. We

3. ____ is a woman.

 a. She   b. He

4. ____ are books.

 a. It   b. They

5. ____ is a signature.

 a. It   b. They

C Complete the sentences. Use *is* or *are*.

1. Mai _____is_____ a student.

2. John _____ a teacher.

3. The teacher _____ a man.

4. You _____ a student.

5. It _____ a student ID.

6. They _____ books.

7. We _____ men.

D Match. Complete the sentences.

_c_ 1. We   a. is a man.

____ 2. He   b. are a woman.

____ 3. I   c. are teachers.

____ 4. It   d. am Kofi.

____ 5. She   e. is a woman.

____ 6. You   f. is my last name.

E 🚀 Grammar Boost   Unscramble the sentences.

1. teacher / is / He / my

   He is my teacher.

2. women / They / are

   _____

3. a / clock / is / It

   _____

4. are / students / We

   _____

5. first / My / name / Rosa / is

   _____

6. man / a / I / am

   _____

A Complete the conversation. Use the words in the box.

| is   you   meet   ~~am~~ |

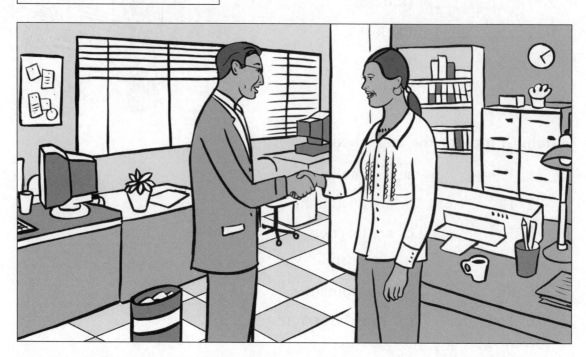

Jin: Hi, I _____am_____ Jin. What is your name?
                    1

Anna: My name _____ Anna.
                          2

Jin: Nice to meet _____.
                              3

Anna: Nice to _____ you, too.
                        4

B Circle the words that start with *m*.

A: Hello. I am (Mal.)

B: Excuse me?

A: Mal. M-A-L.

B: Hi. I am Mary.

C Match the questions with the answers.

__c__ 1. Hi, I am Lorena. What is your name?   a. Sal. S-A-L.

____ 2. Excuse me?   b. Nice to meet you, too.

____ 3. Nice to meet you.   c. My name is Sal.

A **Read the list.**

Milford Adult School
Teacher: Carla Boatman
Student: Leo Salas

School supplies

a binder
two pens
an English dictionary
a notebook
two pencils
an eraser

B **Look at A. Circle *a* or *b*.**

1. a. paper   (b.) two pens

2. a. a pencil   b. two pencils

3. a. an eraser   b. a student ID

4. a. two binders   b. an English dictionary

5. a. a binder   b. a book

6. a. two notebooks   b. a notebook

7. a. Milford Adult School   b. Adams Adult School

8. a. Carla Boatman is a student.   b. Carla Boatman is a teacher.

9. a. Leo Salas is a student.   b. Leo Salas is a teacher.

A **Circle the words in the puzzle. Use the words in the box.**

~~open~~	close	sign	last name	she	nice
meet	notebook	eraser	check	binder	circle

```
S  I  G  N  K  I  S  I  S  L (O  P  E  N) A
H  A  X  M  P  E  N  C  I  L  A  Z  M  I  D
E  M  I  X  A  D  I  Y  C  H  E  C  K  M  Z
D  K  M  I  A  P  C  Q  U  N  D  E  R  R  E
C  Z  F  R  M  E  E  R  A  S  E  R  U  M  L
M  E  E  T  M  Z  D  F  R  A  I  H  T  J  T
C  T  R  U  M  D  E  R  N  L  J  A  R  W  E
L  A  S  T  N  A  M  E  C  O  R  Z  P  R  H
F  R  A  U  P  A  A  E  L  Z  R  R  C  M  R
C  B  I  N  D  E  R  S  O  Z  R  A  R  M  A
P  I  N  D  E  S  R  D  S  A  F  D  L  K  E
C  A  R  C  D  N  O  T  E  B  O  O  K  A  C
```

B **Complete the words in each sentence with one letter.**
Use the letters in the box.

a	e	~~i~~	o	u

1. C__i__rcle number f__i__ve.

2. Nic____ to m____ ____t you.

3. My first n____me is Roxana.

4. They are my n____teb____ ____ks.

5. Yo____ are a st____dent.

UNIT 2

How are you feeling?

LESSON 1 Vocabulary

A Match the words with the pictures. Use the words in the box.

~~fine~~	happy	sad	excited	hungry	tired	thirsty	sick

1. _____**fine**_____

2. _____

3. _____

4. _____

5. _____

6. _____

7. _____

8. _____

B Look at the chart. Circle *yes* or *no*.

1. Jerry is tired.   (yes)   no
2. Joan is hungry.   yes   no
3. Corbin is happy.   yes   no
4. Kathy is sad.   yes   no

Name	Feeling
Jerry	tired
Joan	excited
Corbin	happy
Kathy	sick

A Look at the form. Complete the sentences. Use the words in the box.

~~Lian Wong~~	happy	Greenville, Texas	China

FENWAY ADULT SCHOOL

Lian Wong
Name

Greenville, Texas
City   State

China
birthplace (country)

1. My name is _____Lian Wong_____.

2. I am from _____.

3. Now I am in _____, _____.

4. I am _____.

B Look at the form in A. Circle *yes* or *no*.

1. Lian is from China.   (yes)   no
2. The city is Texas.   yes   no
3. The state is Greenville.   yes   no
4. She is sad.   yes   no

A Complete the sentences. Circle *a* or *b*.

1. She ____ hungry.

   (a.) is not   b. are not

2. You ____ happy.

   a. is not   b. are not

3. The students ____ thirsty.

   a. is not   b. are not

4. Lam ____ sick.

   a. is not   b. are not

5. We ____ sad.

   a. is not   b. are not

6. Anita ____ tired.

   a. is not   b. are not

B Look at the pictures. Complete the sentences. Use *is, is not, are,* or *are not*.

1. She ____is not____ sick.

2. He _____ hungry.

3. They _____ happy.

4. Sal _____ tired.

5. Inez _____ tired.

6. They _____ thirsty.

C Match. Complete the sentences.

_b_ 1. She   a. are not tired.

____ 2. I   b. is not hungry.

____ 3. We   c. am not sad.

D Complete the sentences. Use *am not, is not,* or *are not*.

1. The students ____are not____ sad.

2. I _____ happy.

3. We _____ hungry.

4. You _____ excited.

5. Chris _____ fine.

6. Marta _____ thirsty.

E Write new sentences. Use contractions for the underlined words.

1. <u>I am</u> excited. _____ I'm excited. _____

2. <u>She is</u> from Haiti. _____

3. <u>You are</u> not thirsty. _____

4. <u>I am</u> from Dallas, Texas. _____

5. <u>They are</u> not hungry. _____

6. <u>We are</u> fine. _____

F Look at the picture. Write sentences. Use *He's* or *He's not* and the words in parentheses.

1. (happy) _____ He's happy. _____

2. (a teacher) _____

3. (in Riverside) _____

G 🚀 **Grammar Boost** Write sentences. Use contractions for the underlined words.

1. <u>She</u> / <u>is</u> / not / tired

   She's not tired. _____

2. <u>I</u> / <u>am</u> / happy

   _____

3. <u>He</u> / <u>is</u> / from / Colorado

   _____

4. <u>We</u> / <u>are</u> / not / hungry

   _____

5. <u>It</u> / <u>is</u> / not / my / book

   _____

6. <u>They</u> / <u>are</u> / sick

   _____

A **Complete the conversation. Use the words in the box.**

| sorry | I'm | ~~are~~ | feeling |

Petra: Hi, Ali. How _____*are*_____ you feeling?
                             1

Ali: I'm fine. How are you _____?
                                      2

Petra: _____ sick.
                  3

Ali: Oh, I'm _____.
                       4

B **Match the questions with the answers.**

_d_ 1. How are you feeling?   a. I'm from Mexico.

____ 2. What's your name?   b. He's from Korea.

____ 3. Where are you from?   c. My name is Zita.

____ 4. How is she feeling?   d. I'm tired.

____ 5. Where is he from?   e. She's fine.

A **Read the envelope.**

Springfield Adult School
38 West Street
Springfield, GA 31329

Luis Salas
1242 Lee Street
Rincon, GA 31326

B **Look at A. Circle *yes* or *no*.**

1. The return address is 38 West Street, Springfield, GA 31329. (yes) no
2. The mailing address is 1242 Lee Street, Rincon, GA 31326. yes no
3. The school is in Springfield. yes no
4. Luis's address is 38 West Street. yes no
5. The school zip code is 31326. yes no
6. Luis's zip code is 31329. yes no

C **Complete the sentences. Use words from the envelope in A.**

1. The school is _____ Springfield Adult School _____.

2. The school's city is _____.

3. The school's zip code is _____.

4. The student is _____.

5. The student's street is _____.

6. The mailing address is _____.

A **Look at the pictures. Match the pictures to the sentences.**

_a_ 1. Leila and Gerry are happy.

____ 2. Leila is tired.

____ 3. Now she is excited.

____ 4. She is sad.

B **Complete the words in each sentence with one letter.**
Use the letters in the box.

a   e   ~~i~~   o   u

1. Camille __i__s from Ha__i__t__i__.

2. Wh____r____ ar____ you from?

3. Ricardo is fr____m C____l____rad____.

4. Yo____ are h____ngry.

5. Wh____t's your n____me?

What time is it?

LESSON 1 Vocabulary

A Match the pictures and the words.

_f_ 1. It's midnight.   ____ 4. It's 8:30.

____ 2. It's 7:30.   ____ 5. It's noon.

____ 3. It's 3:00.   ____ 6. It's 6:00.

B Look at the pictures in A. Complete the words.

1. m o _r_ _n_ i _n_ g

2. n ____ ____ n

3. a ____ t ____ ____ ____ ____ o n

4. e ____ ____ ____ i ____ g

5. n ____ ____ ____ ____

6. m ____ d ____ ____ ____ ____ ____

A Look at the pictures. Complete the sentences. Use the words in the box.

| ~~work~~ | English class | home | clinic | store | library | school |

1. I go to _____work_____ at 7:30.

2. I go to the _____ at 3:30.

3. I go to the _____ at 4:30.

4. I go to the _____ at 5:00.

5. I go to _____ at 6:30.

6. I go to _____ at 7:00.

7. I go _____ at 9:00.

B Complete the chart. Use the times in the box.

| ~~8:00 a.m.~~ | ~~4:00 p.m.~~ | 1:30 p.m. | 10:30 a.m. | 2:15 p.m. | 7:45 a.m. |

Morning	Afternoon
8:00 a.m.	4:00 p.m.

A **Complete the questions. Use *Is* or *Are*.**

1. _____*Is*_____ she at work?

2. _____ you at the store?

3. _____ David at the library?

4. _____ they at the clinic?

5. _____ it 3:15?

B **Match the pictures and the questions.**

__*c*__ 1. Is she at home?

_____ 2. Is he at the store?

_____ 3. Are you at school?

_____ 4. Are they at the library?

C **Complete the questions and answers. Circle *a* or *b*.**

1. Is it 2:00 ____

   (a.)?   b. .

2. She's at the clinic ____

   a. ?   b. .

3. Is he at home ____

   a. ?   b. .

4. Is it midnight ____

   a. ?   b. .

5. They're in English class ____

   a. ?   b. .

6. He's at work ____

   a. ?   b. .

D Complete the conversations. Use *am*, *is*, or *are*.

1. A: Are they at work?   B: Yes, they ____are____.

2. A: Is Gary at home?   B: Yes, he _____.

3. A: Is it 3:30?   B: Yes, it _____.

4. A: Are you at the store?   B: Yes, I _____.

5. A: Are we tired?   B: Yes, we _____.

6. A: Is she at school?   B: Yes, she _____.

E Write new sentences. Use contractions for the underlined words.

1. No, they are not.   No, they're not. _____

2. No, we are not.   _____

3. No, I am not.   _____

4. No, it is not.   _____

5. No, she is not.   _____

6. No, he is not.   _____

F Grammar Boost Read the answers. Then write *Yes/No* questions. Use the words in parentheses.

1. (Emily / Georgia)

   A: _Is Emily from Georgia?_____

   B: No, she's not.

2. (Susan / sick)

   A: _____

   B: Yes, she is.

3. (the students / English class)

   A: _____

   B: Yes, they are.

4. (you / library)

   A: _____

   B: No, I'm not.

5. (it / 6:45)

   A: _____

   B: No, it's not.

A **Complete the conversation. Use the words and time in the box.**

library	is	10:00	~~time~~

Pao: Excuse me. What ___time___ is it?
                          1

Diego: It's _____ .
                      2

Pao: Is the _____ open?
                    3

Diego: Yes, it _____ .
                      4

B **Match the questions with the answers.**

__d__ 1. What's your name?   a. I'm from Colorado.

____ 2. Are you a student?   b. It's 4:30.

____ 3. Where are you from?   c. Yes, I am.

____ 4. Is the school open?   d. My name is Pilar.

____ 5. What time is it?   e. Yes, it is.

LESSON 5 **Real-life reading**

A Read the train schedule.

Train Number	Helen	Fenway	River City	Maple
55	8:00 a.m.	8:20 a.m.	9:30 a.m.	11:00 a.m.
86	1:00 p.m.	1:20 p.m.	——————	4:15 p.m.
10	3:30 p.m.	——————	5:00 p.m.	6:30 p.m.
25	5:00 p.m.	5:20 p.m.	6:30 p.m.	8:00 p.m.

B Look at A. Circle *yes* or *no*.

1. Train 55 is at Fenway. Is it 8:20 a.m.? (yes) no

2. Train 25 is at Helen. Is it 6:30 p.m.? yes no

3. Train 86 is at Maple. Is it 4:15 p.m.? yes no

4. Train 10 is at River City. Is it 5 p.m.? yes no

A **Complete the sentences. Use the words in the box.**

| noon | minutes | midnight | ~~home~~ | train | time | morning | evening |

Across

1. Is Mona at _____?

4. The _____ is at Fenway at 1:20 p.m.

5. The store is open at _____.

6. At 12 a.m., it is _____.

8. The trip is 30 _____.

Down

2. English class is a night class. It's in the _____.

3. I go to work in the _____.

7. What _____ is it?

B **Write the words in the crossword puzzle.**

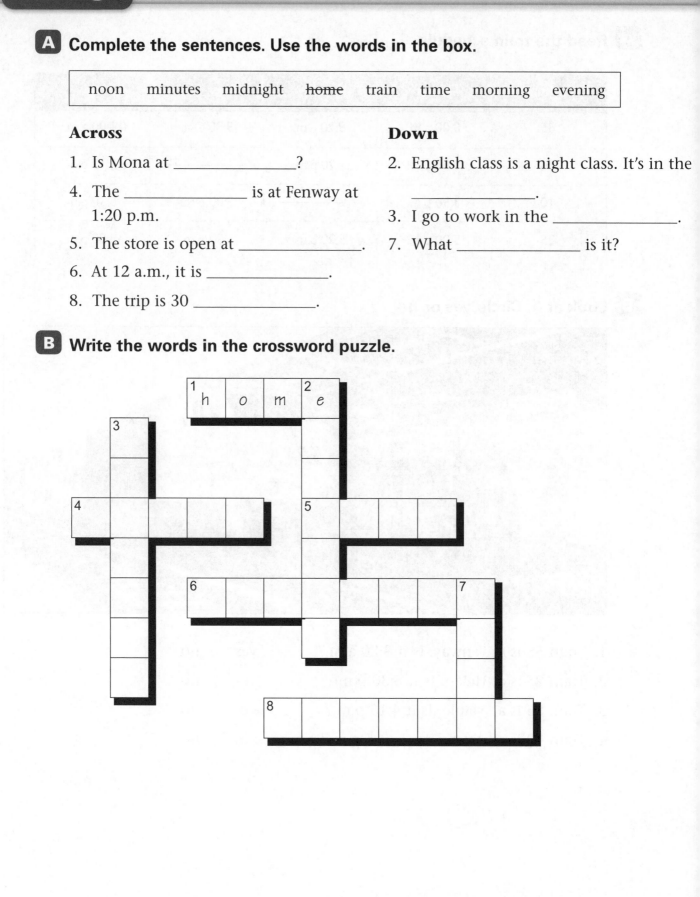

What day is it?

Vocabulary

A Look at the picture. Write the missing letters.

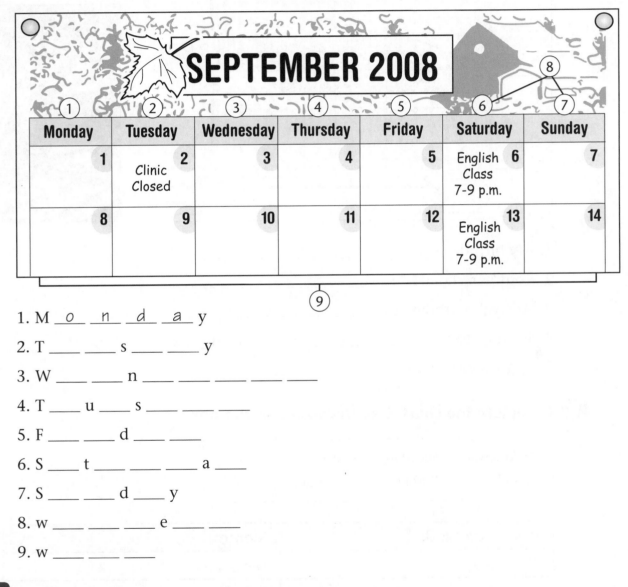

1. M _o_ _n_ _d_ _a_ y
2. T ___ ___ s ___ ___ y
3. W ___ ___ n ___ ___ ___ ___ ___
4. T ___ u ___ s ___ ___ ___
5. F ___ ___ d ___ ___
6. S ___ t ___ ___ ___ a ___
7. S ___ ___ d ___ y
8. w ___ ___ ___ e ___ ___
9. w ___ ___ ___

B Look at the picture in A. Circle *yes* or *no*.

1. Today is Tuesday. Tomorrow is Wednesday.   (yes)   no
2. The clinic is closed on Thursday.   yes   no
3. English class is on Monday and Wednesday.   yes   no
4. Today is Friday. Tomorrow is Saturday.   yes   no

A Look at the picture. Complete the sentences. Use the words in the box.

~~May~~	June	month	August	July

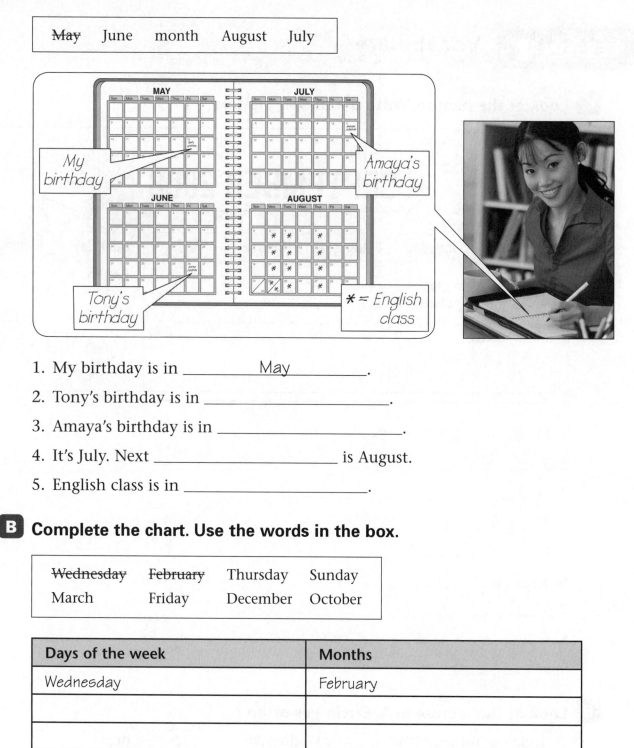

1. My birthday is in _____ May _____.

2. Tony's birthday is in _____.

3. Amaya's birthday is in _____.

4. It's July. Next _____ is August.

5. English class is in _____.

B Complete the chart. Use the words in the box.

~~Wednesday~~	~~February~~	Thursday	Sunday
March	Friday	December	October

Days of the week	Months
Wednesday	February

A **Complete the sentences. Circle *a* or *b*.**

1. The party is ____ Friday.

   (a.) on   b. at

2. School is ____ Tuesdays and Thursdays.

   a. on   b. at

3. English class is ____ 7:00.

   a. on   b. at

4. The birthday party is ____ 8:00.

   a. on   b. at

5. I go to work ____ 7 a.m.

   a. on   b. at

6. I go to the library ____ Saturdays.

   a. on   b. at

B **Look at the pictures. Write two sentences about each picture. Use *on* or *at* and the words and times in parentheses.**

1. (Wednesday)

   The class party is on Wednesday.

2. (3:00)

   _____

3. (Saturday)

   _____

4. (5:00)

   _____

C Complete the conversation. Use *What*, *Where*, or *When*.

1. A: ___Where___ is the party?

   B: It's at school.

2. A: _____ is the party?

   B: It's on Friday.

3. A: _____ time is the party?

   B: It's at noon.

D Match the questions with the answers.

__d__ 1. When is the birthday party?   a. It's at 6:30.

____ 2. When is English class?   b. It's on Mondays.

____ 3. What time is English class?   c. Yes, I am!

____ 4. Is English class on Wednesdays?   d. It's on Saturday.

____ 5. Where is the birthday party?   e. Yes, it is.

____ 6. Are you excited?   f. It's at Atlanta Pizza.

E 🚀 **Grammar Boost** Unscramble the sentences.

1. party / 8:00 / class / The / at / is

   ___The class party is at 8:00.___

2. class / My / School / is / Adult / at / Maple

   _____

3. The / birthday / Tuesday / party / on / is

   _____

4. house / at / my / party / is / The

   _____

5. Thursday / on / class / is / English

   _____

6. birthday / January / in / My / is

   _____

A **Complete the conversation. Use the words and time in the box.**

| Thursday | Goodbye | 9:00 | ~~What~~ |

Alfredo: ___What___ time is it?
             1

Deenah: It's _____.
            2

Alfredo: Thanks. _____. Have a nice evening.
             3

Deenah: Thanks. You, too. See you _____.
             4

B **Circle the words that start with w.**

A: Excuse me. (When) is the class party?

B: It's on Wednesday.

A: Thanks. Have a nice weekend.

B: You, too. See you next week.

A Read the class calendar.

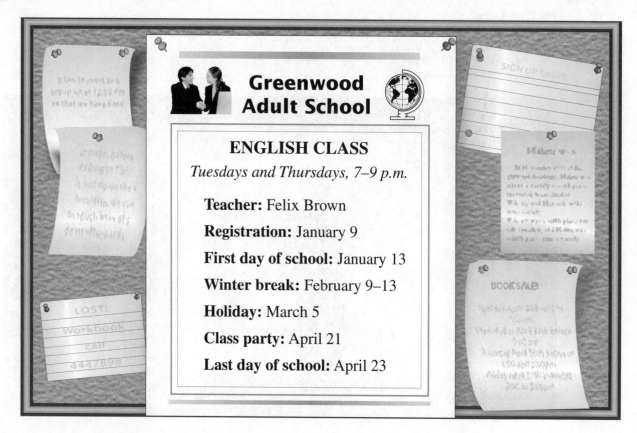

B Look at the class calendar in A. Complete the sentences.

1. Registration is _____January 9_____.

2. Winter break is from February _____ to February _____.

3. _____ is the class party.

4. The last day of school is _____.

5. English class is on Tuesdays and _____.

C Look at A. Circle *yes* or *no*.

1. The teacher is Felix Greenwood.   yes   (no)
2. English class is from 7–9 p.m.   yes   no
3. The first day of school is January 14.   yes   no
4. The class party is in February.   yes   no
5. Registration is on Tuesdays and Thursdays.   yes   no
6. The holiday is on March 5.   yes   no

A Circle the words in the puzzle. Use the words in the box.

September	registration	weekend	~~month~~	second	where
Thanksgiving	October	goodbye	when	today	seventh

```
A  M  X  R  E  G  I  S  T  R  A  T  I  O  N
(M  O  N  T  H) E  D  G  O  O  K  Z  N  B  P
W  C  R  L  S  C  L  T  M  A  B  R  A  X  Y
C  T  N  D  E  R  E  W  E  E  K  E  N  D  W
M  O  O  P  C  X  M  S  I  R  U  S  I  Y  S
S  B  A  T  O  D  A  Y  W  R  K  O  P  N  E
D  E  E  M  N  E  N  D  E  M  F  S  C  H  V
T  R  I  M  D  J  Y  L  U  A  B  O  O  L  E
Q  D  E  C  O  W  W  H  E  R  E  K  L  E  N
T  H  A  N  K  S  G  I  V  I  N  G  H  U  T
P  A  A  M  O  P  R  J  N  B  R  I  G  N  H
T  S  E  P  T  E  M  B  E  R  V  A  W  L  L
B  D  A  R  W  O  H  N  I  B  O  R  H  M  E
E  Z  O  D  S  X  G  O  O  D  B  Y  E  E  H
R  E  I  T  R  A  Y  D  R  O  G  P  N  N  O
```

B Complete the words in each sentence with one letter. Use the letters in the box.

a	e	~~i~~	o	u

1. Have a n__i__ce even__i__ng.

2. T____m____rr____w is M____nday.

3. S____ ____ ____ you in S____pt____mb____r.

4. Registration is on T____esday, Jan____ary 13, and Th____rsday, Jan____ary 15.

5. The p____rty is on S____turd____y, M____y 23.

How much is it?

Vocabulary

A Match the words with the picture.

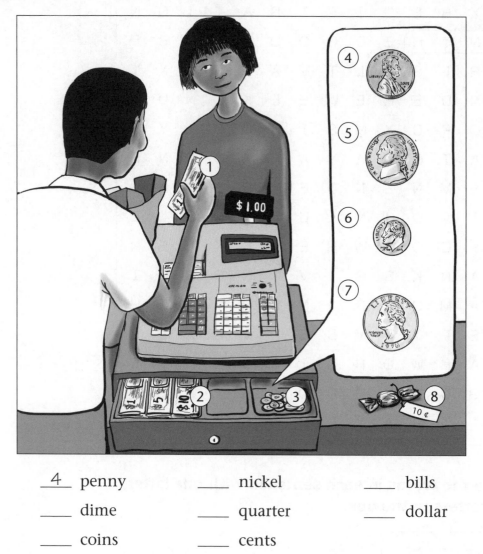

<u>4</u> penny   ____ nickel   ____ bills

____ dime   ____ quarter   ____ dollar

____ coins   ____ cents

B Look at the list. Match the school supplies to the price.

<u>b</u> 1. notebook   a. 99¢

____ 2. two pencils   b. $3

____ 3. book   c. 80¢

____ 4. binder   d. $10

Notebook	$3
Two pencils	80¢
Book	$10
Binder	99¢

A Look at the picture. Complete the sentences. Use the words in the box.

| shirt | ~~sweater~~ | pants | socks | cheap | expensive |

1. The _____sweater_____ is $100.

2. The _____ are $80.50.

3. The _____ are $7.

4. The _____ is $175.

5. The shoes are _____.

6. The skirt is _____.

B Look at the picture in A. Circle *yes* or *no*.

1. The store is River City Clothes.   (yes)   no
2. The women are at home.   yes   no
3. The store is open on Sundays.   yes   no
4. The shoes are cheap.   yes   no

A Look at the pictures. Complete the sentences. Use *This* or *That*.

1. _____This_____ shirt is $10.

2. _____ shirt is $20.

3. _____ book is $21.95.

4. _____ book is $16.

B Complete the sentences. Circle *a* or *b*.

1. ____ computer is $450.

   a. This   b. That

3. ____ computer is $500.

   a. This   b. That

2. ____ notebook is $1.75.

   a. This   b. That

4. ____ notebook is $2.

   a. This   b. That

C Look at the pictures. Write sentences. Use *These* or *Those* and the words in parentheses.

1. ($35) <u>These pants are $35.</u>

2. ($80) _____

3. (expensive) _____

4. ($5) _____

5. (cheap) _____

6. ($15) _____

D Match the pictures and the sentences.

_c_ 1. These shoes are $30.

____ 2. Those shoes are $86.50.

____ 3. These chairs are $199.

____ 4. Those chairs are $250.

____ 5. These clocks are $34.99.

____ 6. Those clocks are $58.

E 🚀 **Grammar Boost** **Complete the sentences. Circle the correct word.**

1. ((That) / Those) student is from Mexico.

2. (This / These) pens are 50¢.

3. (That / Those) sweaters are expensive.

4. (This / These) English class is on Monday.

5. (That / Those) socks are $2.

A Complete the conversation. Use the words and price in the box.

$36	much	It's	Thanks	~~pants~~

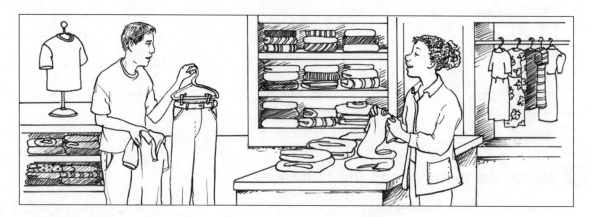

Arun: Excuse me. How much are these ___pants___?
                                                1

Sharon: They're _____.
                            2

Arun: How _____ is this shirt?
                      3

Sharon: _____ $28.25.
                  4

Arun: _____.
              5

B **Real-life math** Look at the picture. Do the math. Then write the sale price.

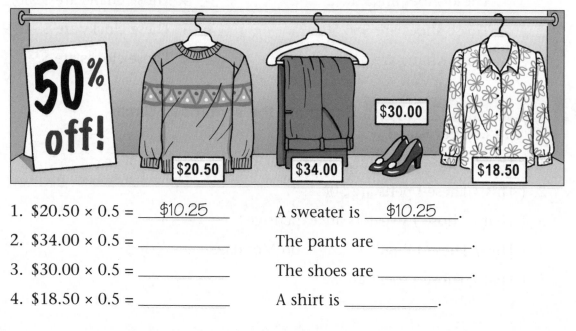

1. $20.50 × 0.5 = ___$10.25___   A sweater is ___$10.25___.

2. $34.00 × 0.5 = _____   The pants are _____.

3. $30.00 × 0.5 = _____   The shoes are _____.

4. $18.50 × 0.5 = _____   A shirt is _____.

A Read the check.

Daniel Robledo, 3619 Helen Street Atlanta, Georgia 30301	3456 DATE 4/30/2009

PAY TO THE ORDER OF __Mapledale Gas Company__ $ __75.54__

__Seventy-five and 54/100__ DOLLARS

FOR __Gas bill__ __Daniel Robledo__

000500321 ":6790046 33': 6721786988""

B Look at the picture in A. Complete the sentences. Circle *a* or *b*.

1. His ____ is $75.54.
   a. gas bill
   b. electric bill

2. The date is ____.
   a. April 30, 2009
   b. January 30, 2009

3. The bill is from ____.
   a. Daniel Robledo
   b. Mapledale Gas Company

4. The amount due is ____.
   a. 3456
   b. $75.54

5. The signature is ____.
   a. Daniel Robledo
   b. gas bill

6. Daniel lives at ____.
   a. 3619 Georgia Street
   b. 3619 Helen Street

7. The zip code is ____.
   a. 30301
   b. 54100

Look at the pictures. Complete the crossword puzzle.

Across

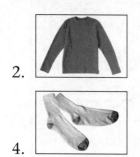

2.

4.

7.

9.

Down

1.

2.

3. $100

5.

6.

8. $8

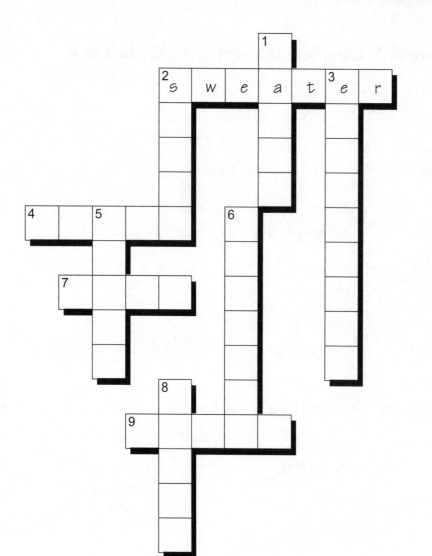

UNIT 6

That's My Son

LESSON 1 **Vocabulary**

 A **Look at the picture. Write the missing letters.**

1. h <u>u</u> s <u>b</u> <u>a</u> <u>n</u> d

2. w ___ ___ e

3. g ___ ___ l

4. b ___ ___

5. m ___ ___ h ___ ___

6. f ___ ___ ___ e ___

7. b ___ ___ ___

8. p ___ r ___ ___ ___ ___

9. f ___ ___ ___ ___ d

B **Look at the chart. Circle _yes_ or _no_.**

			Name	Family Member
1. Is Gloria the mother?	yes	(no)	Joel	father
2. Is Joel the father?	yes	no	Debbie	mother
3. Is Debbie the baby?	yes	no	Gloria	baby
4. Is Sam the friend?	yes	no	Sam	friend

A Look at the pictures. Complete the sentences. Use the words in the box.

| daughter | son | ~~children~~ | sister | brother |

1. These are my _____children_____.

2. This is my _____. He's ten years old.

3. This is my _____. She's six years old.

4. That's my _____. She's married.

5. That's my _____. He's single.

B Look at the picture in A. Circle *yes* or *no*.

1. Are Ivan and Alma divorced?   yes   (no)

2. Is George ten years old?   yes   no

3. Is Alma the wife?   yes   no

4. Is Ivan six years old?   yes   no

A Look at the picture. Complete the sentences. Use *his*, *her*, or *their*.

Name: *Corvin and Abena Kirkwood*
Phone number: *702-555-4590* ④

1. It's _____ his _____ book.

2. It's _____ ID.

3. It's _____ money.

4. It's _____ phone number.

5. It's _____ pen.

B Complete the sentences. Circle *a* or *b*.

1. This is my brother. ____ name is Tom.

  ⓐ His   b. Her

2. She is in my class. ____ name is Ana.

  a. His   b. Her

3. My name is Carlos. What is ____ name?

  a. your   b. my

4. They are my friends. ____ names are Mel and Sandy.

  a. Our   b. Their

5. We are husband and wife. ____ names are Mr. and Mrs. Wong.

  a. Our   b. Their

C **Complete the conversations. Use the verb *live*.**

1. **A:** Is your father in Georgia?

   B: No, he ____lives____ in California.

2. **A:** Are your children in Texas?

   B: Yes, they _____ in Dallas.

3. **A:** Is your friend in Minnesota?

   B: No, she _____ in Haiti.

D **Complete the sentences. Use *live* or *lives*.**

1. Brigitte ____lives____ in Minnesota.

2. Calvin _____ in Washington.

3. You _____ in San Diego.

4. I _____ in Texas.

5. We _____ in Maple.

6. Mr. and Mrs. Levitt _____ in Clinton.

E 🚀 **Grammar Boost** **Write sentences. Use the simple present.**

1. Her / brother / live / in / Florida

   _Her brother lives in Florida._____

2. Our / parents / live / in / Korea

   _____

3. My / daughter / live / in / Colorado

   _____

4. His / sister / live / in / North Carolina

   _____

5. Their / mother / live / in / New York

   _____

6. Your / son / live / in / Haiti

   _____

A Complete the conversation. Use the words in the box.

~~Who's~~	What's	my	name

Tuan: _____Who's_____ that?
              1

Joe: That's _____ son.
                      2

Tuan: _____ his name?
                 3

Joe: His _____ is Tony.
                    4

B 🖩 **Real-life math** Do the math and complete the sentence.

```
|1  |2  |3  |4  |5  |6  |7  |8  |9  |10 |11 |12
```
12 inches = 1 foot

His daughter is three years old.

She is 39 inches tall.

His daughter is _____ feet

and _____ inches tall.

A **Read the note.**

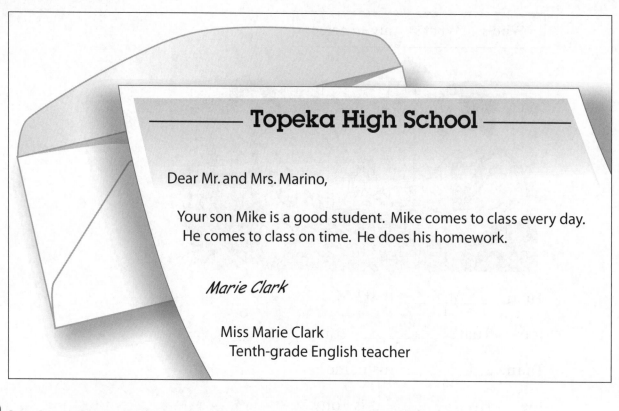

Topeka High School

Dear Mr. and Mrs. Marino,

Your son Mike is a good student. Mike comes to class every day.
He comes to class on time. He does his homework.

Marie Clark

Miss Marie Clark
Tenth-grade English teacher

B **Look at the note in A. Complete the sentences.**

1. Miss Clark is a _____tenth_____-grade teacher.

2. Mike Marino is in _____ school.

3. Mike _____ to class on time.

4. He is a _____ student.

5. Mike does his _____.

A Complete the sentences. Use the words in the box.

| parents baby sister single every day lives Mrs. friend wife |

Across

2. My mother and father are my _____.

5. _____ Vega is a student.

7. Her son _____ in Atlanta.

8. This is my _____, and these are our children.

9. Mike comes to school _____.

Down

1. The _____ is three months old.

3. Silvia is _____.

4. Greg is my _____.

6. They are brother and _____.

B Write the words in the crossword puzzle.

Do we need apples?

Vocabulary

A **Match the words with the pictures. Use the words in the box.**

apples	~~bananas~~	broccoli	fruit	cabbage
corn	grapes	vegetables	oranges	

Grocery

$1.20 50¢ $3 65¢ $1 45¢ $1.30

1 2 3 4 5 6 7

8 9

1. ___bananas___   4. _____   7. _____

2. _____   5. _____   8. _____

3. _____   6. _____   9. _____

B **Look at the picture in A. Complete the questions.**

1. A: How much is the ___broccoli___?

   B: It's $1.30.

2. A: How much are the _____?

   B: They're $1.20.

3. A: How much are the _____?

   B: They're 50¢.

4. A: How much is the _____?

   B: It's 45¢.

A Look at the picture. Complete the sentences. Use the words in the box.

| rice | beef | chicken | ~~lamb~~ | vegetables |

1. The father likes _____lamb_____.

2. The mother likes _____.

3. The daughter likes _____.

4. The son likes _____.

5. They all like _____.

B Complete the chart. Use the words in the box.

| ~~broccoli~~ | ~~apples~~ | ~~beef~~ | oranges | lamb |
| corn | bananas | chicken | cabbage | |

Fruit	Vegetable	Meat
apples	broccoli	beef

A **Complete the sentences. Use _don't_ or _doesn't_.**

1. My parents _____don't_____ like pizza.

2. They _____ like cheese.

3. She _____ like milk.

4. The children _____ like meat.

5. He _____ like vegetables.

6. Her daughter _____ like rice.

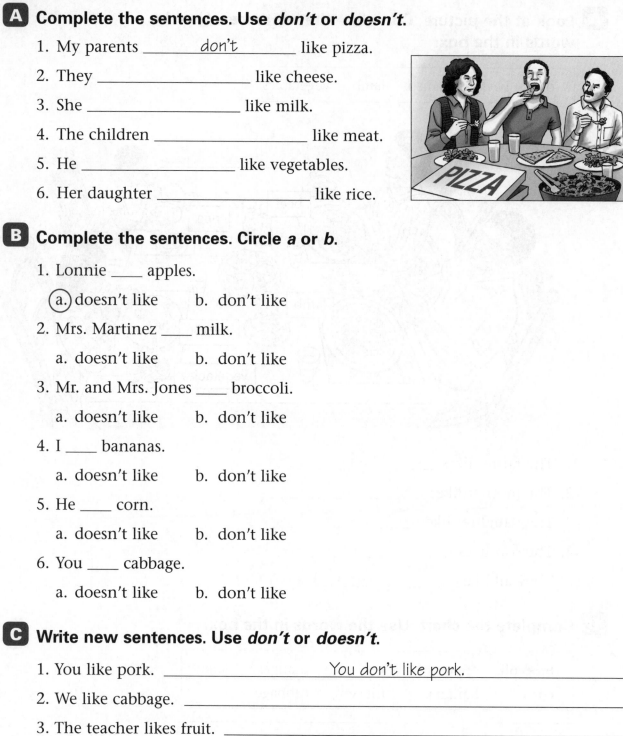

B **Complete the sentences. Circle _a_ or _b_.**

1. Lonnie _____ apples.

   (a.) doesn't like   b. don't like

2. Mrs. Martinez _____ milk.

   a. doesn't like   b. don't like

3. Mr. and Mrs. Jones _____ broccoli.

   a. doesn't like   b. don't like

4. I _____ bananas.

   a. doesn't like   b. don't like

5. He _____ corn.

   a. doesn't like   b. don't like

6. You _____ cabbage.

   a. doesn't like   b. don't like

C **Write new sentences. Use _don't_ or _doesn't_.**

1. You like pork. _____ You don't like pork. _____

2. We like cabbage. _____

3. The teacher likes fruit. _____

4. I like lamb. _____

5. The boy likes bread. _____

D **Complete the conversations. Use _do_ or _does_.**

1. **A:** Do we need eggs?

   B: Yes, we _____ do _____.

2. **A:** Does she need fruit?

   B: Yes, she _____.

3. **A:** Do you need beef?

   B: Yes, I _____.

4. **A:** Do they need vegetables?

   B: Yes, they _____.

5. **A:** Does he need corn?

   B: Yes, he _____.

E **Match the questions with the answers.**

_d_ 1. Does Alonso need a notebook?

____ 2. Does Tina need pencils?

____ 3. Do we need apples?

____ 4. Do I need bread?

____ 5. Do Mr. and Mrs. Winters need rice?

a. No, they don't.

b. No, she doesn't.

c. Yes, you do.

d. No, he doesn't.

e. No, we don't.

F 🚀 **Grammar Boost** **Unscramble the sentences.**

1. grapes / doesn't / Raja / like

   Raja doesn't like grapes.

2. need / students / The / English / an / dictionary

   _____

3. Reza / Ms. / oranges / needs

   _____

4. in / live / don't / We / Washington

   _____

5. children / eggs / The / like / don't

   _____

6. like / don't / chicken / You

   _____

A Put the conversation in the correct order.

____ **Fatima:** Thanks.

____ **Paul:** Here you go.

__1__ **Fatima:** Excuse me. I need milk and eggs.

____ **Paul:** You're welcome.

B **Real-life math** Read the problems. Do the math.
Write the prices.

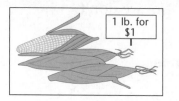

1. We need 3 pounds of corn.

   1 lb. × __3__ = 3 lbs.

   $1 × 3 = $_3_

   3 lbs. of corn = $_3_

3. You need 3 pounds of apples.

   1 lb. × ____ = 3 lbs.

   $2 × 3 = $____

   3 lbs. of apples = $____

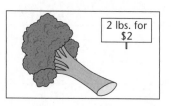

2. She needs 4 pounds of broccoli.

   2 lbs. × ____ = 4 lbs.

   $2 × 2 = $____

   4 lbs. of broccoli = $____

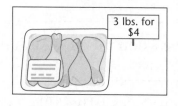

4. I need 6 pounds of chicken.

   3 lbs. × ____ = 6 lbs.

   $4 × 2 = $____

   6 lbs. of chicken = $____

A **Read the shopping list.**

Shopping list

cereal – 2 boxes
tea – 1 box
water – 6 bottles
oranges – 3 pounds
chicken – 2 pounds
soup – 3 cans
milk
cheese – 1 pound

B **Look at A. Circle *yes* or *no*.**

1. Does Mrs. Ma need oranges?   (yes)   no
2. Does she need 6 bottles of water?   yes   no
3. Does she need 4 pounds of chicken?   yes   no
4. Does she need 5 cans of soup?   yes   no
5. Does Mrs. Ma need beef?   yes   no
6. Does she need 1 box of tea?   yes   no

C **Complete the sentences. Use words from the list in A.**

1. Mrs. Ma needs 2 boxes of _____cereal_____.

2. She needs 3 pounds of _____.

3. She needs 2 pounds of _____.

4. Mrs. Ma needs _____ bottles of water.

5. She needs _____ pound of cheese.

6. She needs _____ cans of soup.

Look at the pictures. Complete the crossword puzzle.

Across

 2.

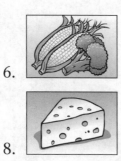 6.

5.

8.

Down

1.

 7.

 9.

3.

4.

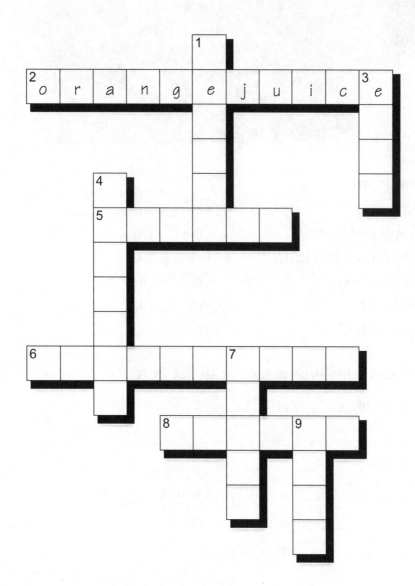

| 2 | o | r | a | n | g | e | | j | u | i | c | 3 | e |

UNIT **8**

Take Two Tablets

LESSON **1**   Vocabulary

A Look at the picture. Write the missing letters.

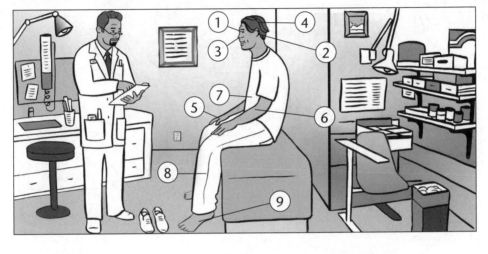

1. e __y__ e

2. e ____ r

3. n ____ s ____

4. h e ____ ____

5. h a ____ ____

6. a ____ ____

7. s ____ ____ ____ ____ c ____

8. l ____ ____

9. f ____ ____ ____

B Look at the form. Circle *yes* or *no*.

1. His first name is Arun.   (yes)   no

2. His address is 60602 Walnut Street.   yes   no

3. His phone number is (312) 555-2390.   yes   no

A Look at the picture. Match the person to the health problem.

_e_ 1. Alicia   a. headache

___ 2. David   b. sore throat

___ 3. Mrs. Laurent   c. fever

___ 4. Mr. Laurent   d. stomachache

___ 5. Barbara   e. cough

___ 6. Patrick   f. earache

B Look at the picture in A. Circle *yes* or *no*.

1. Barbara has a stomachache.   (yes)   no
2. Mr. Laurent has the flu.   yes   no
3. David has a fever.   yes   no
4. Mrs. Laurent has an earache.   yes   no
5. Alicia has a cough.   yes   no
6. Patrick has an earache.   yes   no

A Look at the pictures. Write 2 sentences about each picture. Use *has* or *have* and the words in parentheses.

1. (I) __I have a sore throat.__

2. (You) _____

3. (She) _____

4. (He) _____

5. (We) _____

6. (They) _____

B Complete the sentences. Use *has* or *have*.

1. His daughter _____ has _____ an earache.

2. Her son _____ the flu.

3. The teacher and the students _____ fevers.

4. My mother _____ a cough.

5. Annie and Daniela _____ sore throats.

6. Their friend _____ a headache.

C Match the questions with the answers.

_c_ 1. Does Patricia have a book?   a. No, they don't.

____ 2. Do Donna and Marcus have children?   b. Yes, we do.

____ 3. Does Azim have a credit card?   c. No, she doesn't.

____ 4. Do you have $20?   d. No, he doesn't.

____ 5. Do we have apples?   e. Yes, I do.

D Complete the conversations. Use *does* or *do*.

1. A: Does he have an earache?   B: Yes, he _____ does _____.

2. A: Does she have a sore throat? B: Yes, she _____.

3. A: Do I have a fever?   B: Yes, you _____.

4. A: Do they have the flu?   B: Yes, they _____.

E Write questions. Use *do* or *does*, *have*, and the words in parentheses.

1. (she, sweater) _____ Does she have a sweater? _____

2. (they, eggs) _____

3. (you, quarter) _____

4. (he, car) _____

5. (we, paper) _____

F 🚀 Grammar Boost   Complete the questions and answers. Use *do*, *does*, *have*, or *has*.

1. A: _____ Does _____ Nancy have a fever?

   B: No, she _____ has _____ an earache.

2. A: _____ he have a stomachache?

   B: No, he _____ a headache.

3. A: _____ Mr. and Mrs. Chavez have the flu?

   B: No, they _____ colds.

4. A: _____ you have a cough?

   B: No, I _____ a sore throat.

5. A: _____ I have the flu?

   B: No, you _____ a cold.

A **Complete the conversation. Use the words and time in the box.**

| thank | 11:00 | name | flu | doctor | Rosita | matter | ~~Hello~~ |

Receptionist: _____Hello_____, River City Clinic.

                          1

Adolfo: This is Adolfo Flores. My daughter needs to see the _____.

                                                                        2

Receptionist: What's the _____?

                                3

Adolfo: She has the _____.

                                4

Receptionist: What's her _____?

                                 5

Adolfo: Her name is _____. She's seven months old.

                                6

Receptionist: Is _____ OK?

                       7

Adolfo: Yes, _____ you.

                           8

B **Circle the words that start with s.**

A: Hi, (Sharon.) Are you at (school?)

B: No, I'm at the clinic in Springfield.

A: Are you sick?

B: Yes, I have a stomachache.

A: Oh, I'm sorry.

B: Thanks. See you next Saturday.

A **Read the forms.**

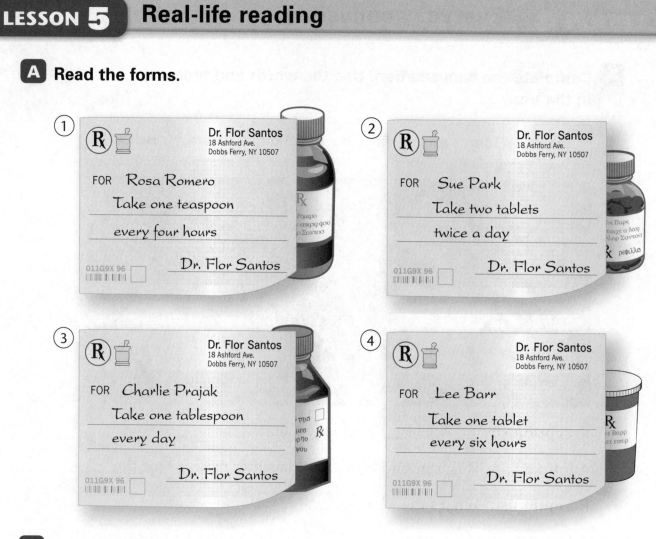

B **Look at A. Circle *a* or *b*.**

1. Medicine 1:

   a. take two teaspoons   b. take one teaspoon

2. Medicine 2:

   a. take three times a day   b. take twice a day

3. Medicine 2:

   a. take two tablets   b. take one tablet

4. Medicine 3:

   a. take one tablespoon   b. take one teaspoon

5. Medicine 4:

   a. take every four hours   b. take every six hours

6. Medicine 4:

   a. take six tablets   b. take one tablet

A Complete the words in each sentence with one letter. Use the letters in the box.

~~a~~ e i o u

1. Wh__a__t's the m__a__tter?

2. Take tw____ tablesp____ ____ns every f____ur h____urs.

3. We have med____c____ne for colds.

4. I n____ ____d to s____ ____ th____ doctor.

5. Do yo____ have the fl____?

B Look at the pictures. Match the pictures to the sentences.

__a__ 1. "You have a fever."

____ 2. "Is 1:00 OK?"

____ 3. "Hello. My daughter needs to see the doctor."

____ 4. "Your daughter has the flu."

____ 5. "Yes, thank you. Goodbye."

What size?

A Complete the chart. Use the words in the box.

| ~~orange~~ ~~pants~~ socks shirt purple red shoes green |

Colors	Clothes
orange	pants

B Complete the color words. Write the missing letters.

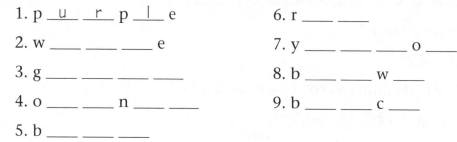

1. p _u_ _r_ p _l_ e

2. w ___ ___ ___ e

3. g ___ ___ ___ ___

4. o ___ ___ n ___ ___

5. b ___ ___ ___

6. r ___ ___

7. y ___ ___ ___ o ___

8. b ___ ___ w ___

9. b ___ ___ c ___

A Look at the pictures. Complete the sentences. Use the words in the box.

| boots | ~~shorts~~ | cap | jacket | dress | belt |

1. **Matt:** I'm wearing _____ shorts _____.
2. **Greg:** I'm wearing a _____.

3. **Nancy:** It's a _____.
4. **Selma:** It's a _____.

5. **Tina:** I'm wearing _____.
6. **Paul:** It's a new _____.

B Look at the pictures in A. Circle *yes* or *no*.

1. Matt is wearing a cap.   yes   (no)
2. Greg is wearing shorts.   yes   no
3. Nancy is wearing pants.   yes   no
4. Selma is wearing a jacket.   yes   no
5. Tina is wearing a coat.   yes   no
6. Paul is wearing a sweater.   yes   no

A Complete the sentences. Use *am, is,* or *are*.

1. He _____is_____ wearing a brown sweater.

2. You _____ wearing a purple T-shirt.

3. Anita _____ wearing a white coat.

4. We _____ wearing green jackets.

5. I _____ wearing a black dress.

6. Norma and Chang Sun _____ wearing blue caps.

B Look at the pictures. Write 3 sentences about each picture. Use *is wearing* or *are wearing* and the words in parentheses.

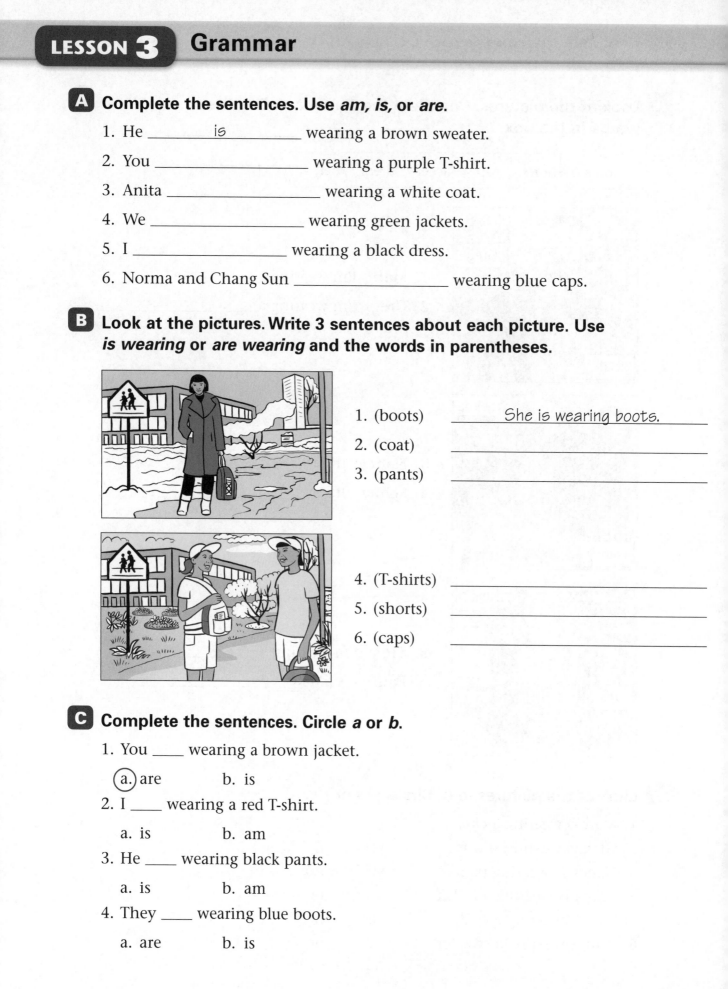

1. (boots) _____She is wearing boots._____

2. (coat) _____

3. (pants) _____

4. (T-shirts) _____

5. (shorts) _____

6. (caps) _____

C Complete the sentences. Circle *a* or *b*.

1. You ____ wearing a brown jacket.

   a. are   b. is

2. I ____ wearing a red T-shirt.

   a. is   b. am

3. He ____ wearing black pants.

   a. is   b. am

4. They ____ wearing blue boots.

   a. are   b. is

D **Complete the conversations. Use *Is* or *Are*.**

1. **A:** _____Is_____ she reading a book?

   B: Yes, she is.

2. **A:** _____ he going to the clinic?

   B: No, he's not.

3. **A:** _____ the cat sleeping?

   B: No, it's not.

4. **A:** _____ you wearing a coat?

   B: No, I'm not.

5. **A:** _____ they going to school?

   B: Yes, they are.

E **Answer the questions. Circle *a* or *b*.**

1. Is Claire wearing a purple dress?

   (a.) Yes, she is.   b. Yes, you are.

2. Are the students doing their homework?

   a. Yes, she is.   b. No, they're not.

3. Is Mr. Foss sleeping?

   a. Yes, he is.   b. Yes, she is.

4. Are we wearing sweaters?

   a. No, we're not.   b. No, they're not.

5. Are you going to the store?

   a. Yes, I am.   b. Yes, you are.

F **Grammar Boost** **Write sentences. Use the present continuous.**

1. We / read / the books

   _We are reading the books._____

2. Lila / sleep

   _____

3. He / wear / black / shoes

   _____

4. They / go / to / a party

   _____

A Put the conversation in the correct order.

____ **Eva:** Medium.

____ **Clerk:** What size?

_1_ **Eva:** I'm looking for a dress.

____ **Eva:** Thanks.

____ **Clerk:** Here's a medium.

B Real-life math   Read the receipt. Answer the questions.

1. How much are the socks? _____ $3.00 _____

2. How much is the T-shirt? _____

3. How much are the pants? _____

4. How much is the tax? _____

C Do the math. Write the total on the receipt.

Clothes Town	
08-11-2010 17:12 0196-020 DEP	
Pants	$ 35.00
Socks	$ 3.00
T-shirt	$ 12.50
Tax 5%	$ 2.53
Total	$_____
CUSTOMER COPY	

A **Read the weather report.**

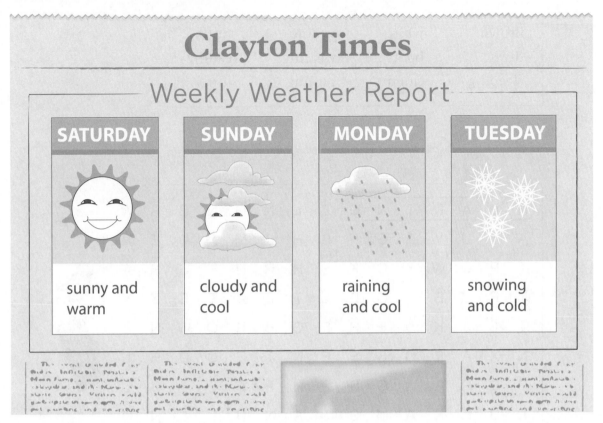

Clayton Times

Weekly Weather Report

SATURDAY	SUNDAY	MONDAY	TUESDAY
sunny and warm	cloudy and cool	raining and cool	snowing and cold

B **Look at A. Circle *a* or *b*.**

1. Saturday

   (a.) sunny   b. cloudy

2. Saturday

   a. warm   b. hot

3. Sunday

   a. sunny   b. cloudy

4. Monday

   a. warm   b. cool

5. Monday

   a. snowing   b. raining

6. Tuesday

   a. snowing   b. raining

C **Complete the sentences. Use words from the weather report in A.**

1. Saturday: _____sunny_____ and warm.

2. Sunday: cloudy and _____.

3. Monday: _____ and cool.

4. Tuesday: snowing and _____.

Circle the words in the puzzle. Use the words in the box.

brown	white	yellow	shorts
dress	boots	wearing	~~reading~~
sleeping	cloudy	raining	sunny

```
R E A D I N G  Z L N G N B R W
A T U Y R G F B H J M X D E R
I P Q W X C K S H R R T S H A
N P M B T O D L I E A T E Z Y
I L J K D E R E G B R O W N E
N X A P O S E E N I E C D R L
G D R A W O S P H F F E J S L
L U E N A M S I A N U L L H O
S R I B D N O N S W C E S O W
G W E A R I N G A L C I T R A
L H A N U F E R I C L V E T S
E I D N S E H T J B O O T S O
N T I O J N O I S C U T R E S
N E R R T D O N I G D A R I M
L A P E S U N N Y E Y N A V Y
```

UNIT 10

Where's the bank?

A Match the pictures with the words.

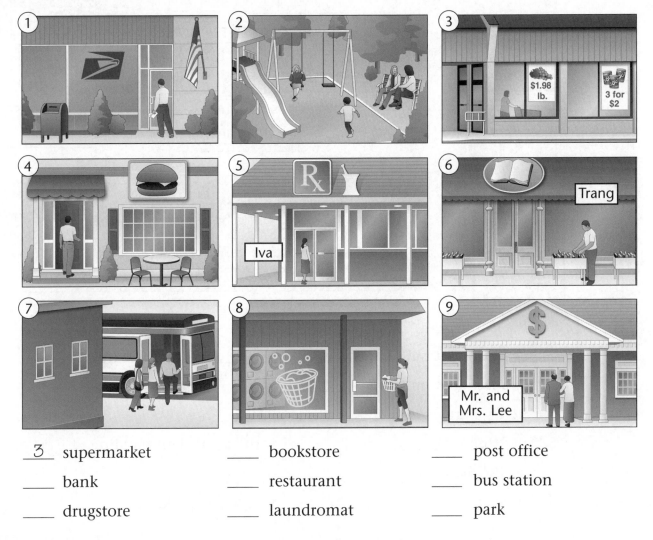

_3_ supermarket   ___ bookstore   ___ post office

___ bank   ___ restaurant   ___ bus station

___ drugstore   ___ laundromat   ___ park

B Look at the pictures in A. Complete the sentences. Use the words in the box.

> ~~park~~   bookstore   bank   drugstore

1. The children like the ____park____.   2. Iva is going to the _____.

3. Trang is at the _____.   4. Mr. and Mrs. Lee are going

         to the _____.

LESSON 2 Life stories

A Look at the picture. Complete the sentences. Use the words in the box.

| on the corner | restaurant | between | ~~apartment building~~ | next to | across from |

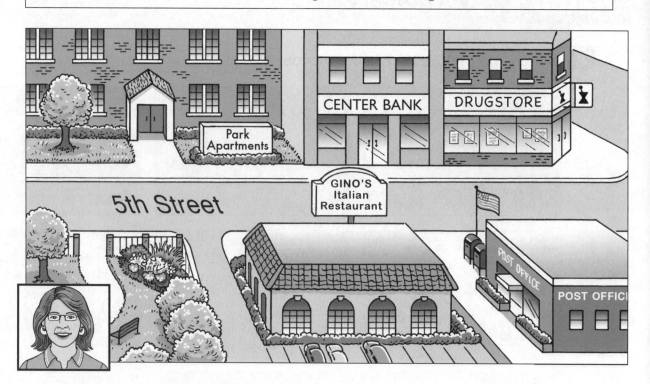

1. This is my __apartment building__.

2. My apartment building is _____ the bank.

3. My apartment building is _____ the park.

4. There's a drugstore _____.

5. The bank is _____ the apartment building and the drugstore.

6. There's a _____ next to the park.

B Look at the picture in A. Circle *yes* or *no*.

1. The bank is on the corner.	yes	(no)
2. There's a laundromat.	yes	no
3. The park is next to the drugstore.	yes	no
4. The street is Fifth Street.	yes	no
5. There's a school.	yes	no
6. The restaurant is between the park and the post office.	yes	no

A **Complete the sentences. Circle *a* or *b*.**

1. There _____ three houses.

    a. is   (b.) are

2. There _____ two laundromats.

    a. is   b. are

3. There _____ an apartment building next to the supermarket.

    a. is   b. are

4. There _____ a clinic across from the library.

    a. is   b. are

5. There _____ a restaurant between the bookstore and the bus station.

    a. is   b. are

B **Look at the picture. Write sentences. Use *There is* or
There are and the words in parentheses.**

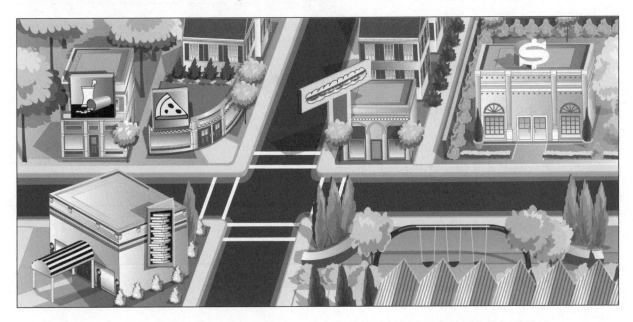

1. (drugstore) <u>There is a drugstore.</u>

2. (restaurants) _____

3. (bank) _____

4. (houses) _____

5. (park) _____

C **Complete the conversations. Use *is* or *isn't*.**

1. **A:** _____Is_____ there a bank on the corner?

   B: Yes, there is.

2. **A:** _____ there a drugstore nearby?

   B: No, there isn't.

3. **A:** Is there a supermarket nearby?

   B: No, there _____.

4. **A:** Is there a restaurant on Walnut Street?

   B: Yes, there _____.

5. **A:** Is there an apartment building across from the post office?

   B: Yes, there _____.

D **Read the sentences. Then write questions.**

1. There's a library nearby. _____*Is there a library nearby?*_____

2. There's an office on the corner. _____

3. There's a park next to the bank. _____

4. There's an elementary school nearby. _____

E  **Grammar Boost** **Unscramble the sentences.**

1. bookstores / There / three / are

   __*There are three bookstores.*_____

2. nearby / bus station / There / is / a

   _____

3. isn't / No, / there

   _____

4. Fifth / Street / There / laundromat / a / is / on

   _____

5. supermarket / nearby / is / a / There

   _____

6. post office / on the corner / is / There / a

   _____

A Put the conversation in the correct order.

____ **Hector:** Thank you.

____ **Vinh:** You're welcome.

____ **Vinh:** Yes, there is. It's between the bank and the bookstore.

__1__ **Hector:** Excuse me. Is there a drugstore nearby?

B **Real-life math** Look at the map. Do the math.
Complete the sentences.

1. Franklin is __7__ miles from Oak Grove.

2. Clayton is ____ miles from Franklin.

3. Clayton is ____ miles from Oak Grove.

A Read the brochure.

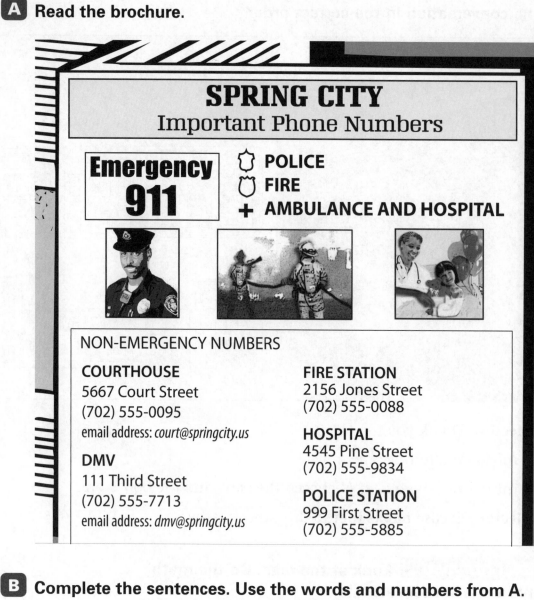

SPRING CITY
Important Phone Numbers

Emergency 911

⬡ POLICE
⬡ FIRE
✚ AMBULANCE AND HOSPITAL

NON-EMERGENCY NUMBERS

COURTHOUSE
5667 Court Street
(702) 555-0095
email address: *court@springcity.us*

DMV
111 Third Street
(702) 555-7713
email address: *dmv@springcity.us*

FIRE STATION
2156 Jones Street
(702) 555-0088

HOSPITAL
4545 Pine Street
(702) 555-9834

POLICE STATION
999 First Street
(702) 555-5885

B Complete the sentences. Use the words and numbers from A.

1. For an emergency, call _____911_____.

2. The non-emergency number for the _____ is
   (702) 555-0088.

3. The non-emergency number for the police station is _____.

4. The DMV is on _____ Street.

5. The email address for the courthouse is _____.

6. The address of the hospital is _____.

7. The email address for the DMV is _____.

8. The police station is on _____ Street.

A Look at the pictures. Match the pictures to the sentences.

  _b_   1. "Hello. 911."

  ____   2. "This is an emergency!"

  ____   3. "Thank you."

  ____   4. "My restaurant is across from the laundromat."

B Complete the words in each sentence with one letter.
Use the letters in the box.

> a   e   i   ~~o~~   u

1. There is a b_o_ _o_kst_o_re acr_o_ss fr_o_m my h_o_use.

2. I go to the p____rk on Mond____ys.

3. Wh____r____ is th____ fir____ station?

4. Is there a dr____gstore next to the co____rtho____se?

5. There are two apartment bu____ld____ngs on th____s street.

UNIT 11

This Is My Home

LESSON 1 Vocabulary

A Match the words with the picture. Use the words in the box.

stove	TV	sofa	~~window~~	room
furniture	refrigerator	bed	dresser	

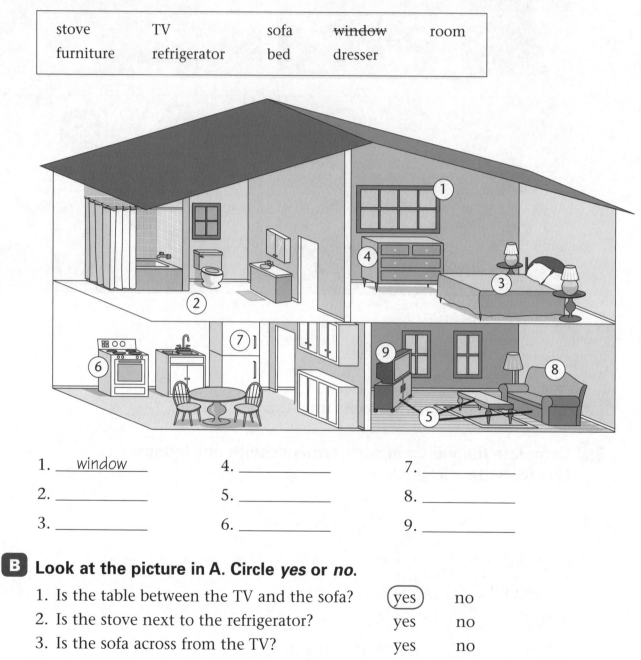

1. _window_
2. _____
3. _____
4. _____
5. _____
6. _____
7. _____
8. _____
9. _____

B Look at the picture in A. Circle *yes* or *no*.

1. Is the table between the TV and the sofa?   (yes)   no
2. Is the stove next to the refrigerator?   yes   no
3. Is the sofa across from the TV?   yes   no
4. Is the dresser next to the bed?   yes   no

A Look at the picture. Complete the sentences. Use the
words in the box.

garage	below	above	in	bedroom	bathroom	on	~~kitchen~~

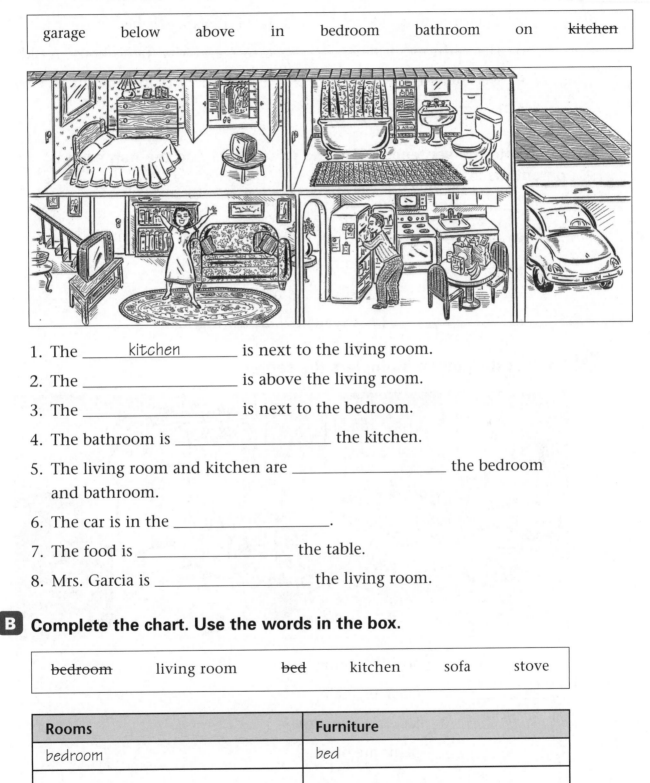

1. The ____kitchen____ is next to the living room.

2. The _____ is above the living room.

3. The _____ is next to the bedroom.

4. The bathroom is _____ the kitchen.

5. The living room and kitchen are _____ the bedroom
   and bathroom.

6. The car is in the _____.

7. The food is _____ the table.

8. Mrs. Garcia is _____ the living room.

B Complete the chart. Use the words in the box.

~~bedroom~~	living room	~~bed~~	kitchen	sofa	stove

Rooms	Furniture
bedroom	bed

A **Match the sentences.**

_d_ 1. Their living room is small.   a. Ethan's kitchen is white.

____ 2. Their house is old.   b. Lisa's garage is big.

____ 3. Her bathroom is blue.   c. Mr. and Mrs. Tam's house is old.

____ 4. His kitchen is white.   d. Ed and Elsa's living room is small.

____ 5. Her garage is big.   e. Jane's bathroom is blue.

B **Complete the sentences. Use the possessive and the names in parentheses.**

1. _____Jia's_____ dress is new. (Jia)

2. _____ bedroom is red. (Mr. and Mrs. Lim)

3. _____ English class is good. (Phu)

4. _____ kitchen is nice. (Kara)

5. _____ sweater is purple. (Ingrid)

C **Look at the picture. Complete the sentences.**

1. _____Galina's_____ dog is sleeping.

2. _____ clock is small.

3. _____ jacket is expensive.

4. _____ pants are black.

D **Complete the questions. Circle a or b.**

1. How many ____ are there in the bedroom?

   a. closet   (b.) closets

2. How many ____ are there?

   a. room   b. rooms

3. How many ____ are there in Claude's house?

   a. bedrooms   b. bedroom

4. How many ____ are there in the bedroom?

   a. windows   b. window

E **Look at the pictures. Write questions and answers.**
Use *How many*.

 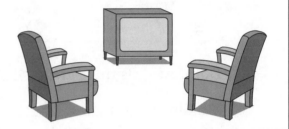

1. How many oranges are there? Three. _____

2. _____

3. _____

4. _____

5. _____

F 🚀 **Grammar Boost**   **Write sentences. Use the possessive.**

1. Mr. and Mrs. Soto / house / is / on the corner

   Mr. and Mrs. Soto's house is on the corner. _____

2. Peng / living room / has / two / sofas

   _____

3. Orane / calendar / is / black and white

   _____

4. Jerry and Olivia / books / are / expensive

   _____

LESSON 4 Everyday conversation

A Complete the conversation. Use the words and price in the box.

there	many	Three	~~apartment~~	rent	$1,100

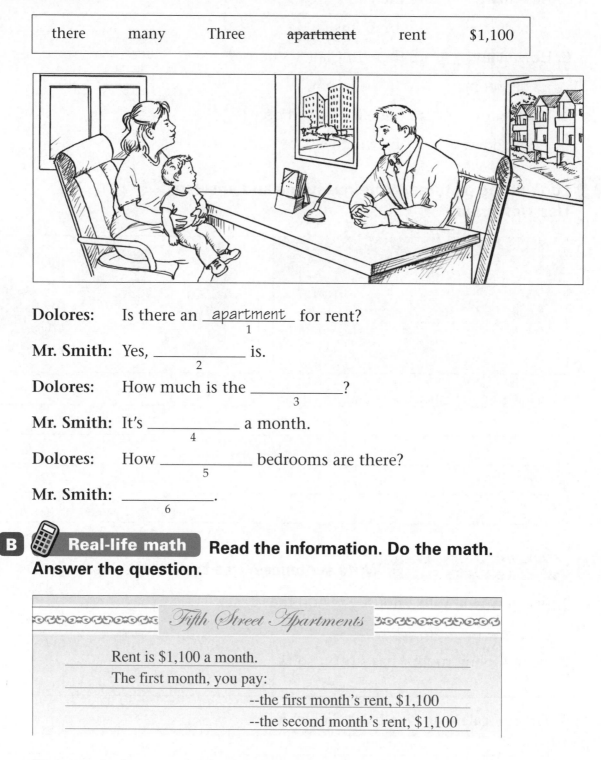

Dolores: Is there an <u>apartment</u> for rent?

                            1

Mr. Smith: Yes, _____ is.

                        2

Dolores: How much is the _____?

                              3

Mr. Smith: It's _____ a month.

                        4

Dolores: How _____ bedrooms are there?

                        5

Mr. Smith: _____.

                  6

B **Real-life math** Read the information. Do the math. Answer the question.

> *Fifth Street Apartments*
>
> Rent is $1,100 a month.
> The first month, you pay:
>   --the first month's rent, $1,100
>   --the second month's rent, $1,100

How much do you pay the first month for this apartment?

$1,100 + $1,100 = $_____

LESSON 5   Real-life reading

A Read the housing ads.

Internet Search

3 BR/3 BA house $1,100 a month
3618 Washington Street   MORE INFO

2 BR/2 BA apartment $850 a month
198 Sixth Street   MORE INFO

Room for rent in my home $425 a month
(240) 555-6795   MORE INFO

2 BR/1 BA duplex $700 a month
9009 Bar Street
(240) 555-83444   MORE INFO

B Look at A. Circle *a* or *b*.

1. How much is the apartment rent?

   a. $425   b. $850

2. How many bedrooms are there in the duplex?

   a. one   b. two

3. Where is the house?

   a. Washington Street   b. Barr Street

4. How many bathrooms are there in the apartment?

   a. one   b. two

5. How much is the room rent?

   a. $425   b. $700

Circle the words in the puzzle. Use the words in the box.

dresser	stove	bedroom	garage
chair	rent	mobile home	window
bathroom	many	apartment	~~kitchen~~

E I T R A S G N O R W I M N T
E S N I D L A R N U F B O C P
N O S K R (K I T C H E N) B D I
E T V A E L H C R A M B I Z O
R O M K S O O S T O V E L R B
N Y L E S L A D T S E R E O E
I M S L E M I W I N D R H J D
E A P A R T M E N T Y E O W R
S U R I S C E X E L S E M Q O
A M A B A T H R O O M P E P O
R W O O E R E H W C H A I R M
E S I O U Y W O N K O H W E R
N R E T G A R A G E H A H T S
T I D R I E O N S L E G G I W
S W I N D O W H I S T M A N Y

Yes, I can!

A Match the words with the pictures.

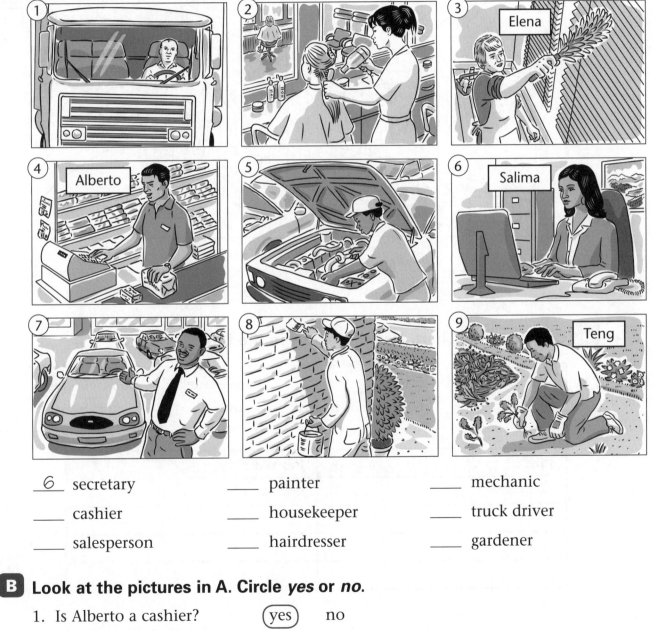

__6__ secretary	____ painter	____ mechanic
____ cashier	____ housekeeper	____ truck driver
____ salesperson	____ hairdresser	____ gardener

B Look at the pictures in A. Circle *yes* or *no*.

1. Is Alberto a cashier?   (yes)   no

2. Is Salima a secretary?   yes   no

3. Is Elena a truck driver?   yes   no

4. Is Teng a painter?   yes   no

A **Look at the picture. Complete the sentences. Use the words in the box.**

use computers	sell clothes	cut hair	~~fix cars~~

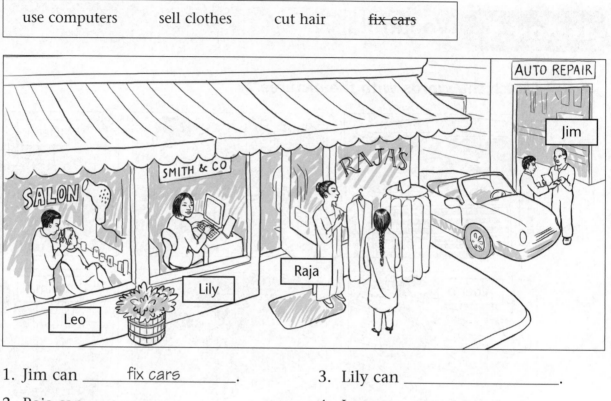

1. Jim can _____ fix cars _____.

2. Raja can _____.

3. Lily can _____.

4. Leo can _____.

B **Complete the chart. Use the words in the box.**

~~truck driver~~	gardener	~~drive trucks~~	housekeeper
clean	take care of plants	painter	paint houses

Jobs	Job skills
truck driver	drive trucks

A **Look at the pictures. Complete the sentences. Use *can* or *can't*.**

1. I _____can_____ fix cars.

2. I _____ fix the computer.

3. Dara _____ fix the computer.

4. Mateo _____ paint houses.

5. He _____ speak English.

6. He _____ drive.

B **Look at the job applications. Write sentences. Use *can* or *can't* and the words in parentheses.**

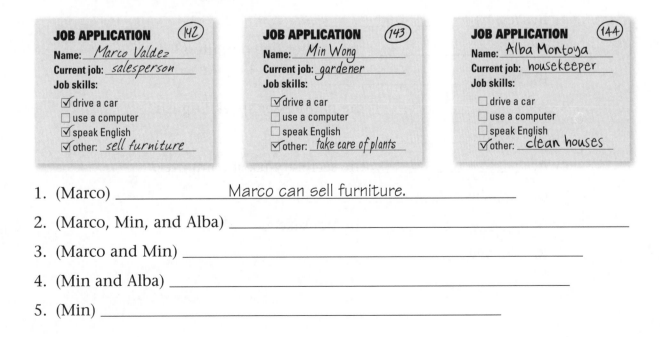

1. (Marco) _____ Marco can sell furniture. _____

2. (Marco, Min, and Alba) _____

3. (Marco and Min) _____

4. (Min and Alba) _____

5. (Min) _____

C **Answer the questions. Circle *a* or *b*.**

1. Can she cut hair?

   a. Yes, he can. (b.) Yes, she can.

2. Can they write in English?

   a. Yes, we can. b. No, they can't.

3. Can you fix cars?

   a. No, I can't. b. No, you can't.

4. Can he paint a house?

   a. No, he can't. b. No, she can't.

5. Can your brother drive a truck?

   a. Yes, you can. b. Yes, he can.

D **Match the questions with the answers.**

_d_ 1. Can you use an English dictionary?   a. Yes, they can.

____ 2. Can Mr. Levitt use the Internet?   b. No, he can't.

____ 3. Can Karen drive a truck?   c. No, he isn't.

____ 4. Can they clean houses?   d. Yes, I can.

____ 5. Is he a salesperson?   e. Yes, she can.

E **Grammar Boost** **Complete the conversations.**
Use *can* or *can't*.

1. A: _____Can_____ the truck driver fix trucks?

   B: Yes, he _____can_____.

2. A: _____ the cashier fix computers?

   B: No, she _____.

3. A: _____ the hairdresser speak English?

   B: Yes, he _____.

4. A: _____ the secretary use a computer?

   B: Yes, she _____.

5. A: _____ the housekeeper drive?

   B: No, she _____.

A Complete the conversation. Use the words in the box.

~~truck~~	can't	Yes	evenings

Mrs. Woods: Can you drive a ____truck____ ?
1

Lionel: _____, I can.
2

Mrs. Woods: Can you work _____?
3

Lionel: No, I _____.
4

B Circle the words that start with *c*.

A: (Can) you use a (computer?)

B: Yes, I can.

A: Can you sell clothes?

B: No, I can't.

A: Can you drive a car?

B: Yes, I can.

A: Can you clean?

B: Yes, I can.

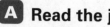

A Read the job ads.

JOBS

Painter

San Diego Painting
FT
Driver's license
Call (619) 555-3477

Classroom Aide

Foss Elementary School
PT
Mornings, Mon.–Fri.
Call (760) 555-6700

Cashier

Your Drugstore
PT, November/December
Nights/weekends
Call (619) 555-0082

Dental Assistant

Dr. Taylor Gilbert
FT
Evenings
Call (858) 555-6432

B Look at A. Circle *a* or *b*.

1. work in the evening

   a. cashier and dental assistant   b. painter and dental assistant

2. work part time in the morning

   a. painter   b. classroom aide

3. work November and December

   a. classroom aide   b. cashier

4. work full time

   a. painter and dental assistant   b. classroom aide and cashier

5. have a driver's license

   a. cashier   b. painter

6. work on Saturdays

   a. cashier   b. dental assistant

A Complete the sentences. Use the words in the box.

babysitter	painter	can	computers	cashier
truck driver	fix	part time	~~housekeeper~~	

Across

2. A _____ can clean.

3. A _____ can paint houses.

6. Yes, I _____.

7. A _____ takes care of children.

8. Melissa is a _____ at the drugstore.

Down

1. Can you use _____?

4. A _____ can drive trucks.

5. Can you work _____?

9. A mechanic can _____ cars.

B Write the words in the crossword puzzle.

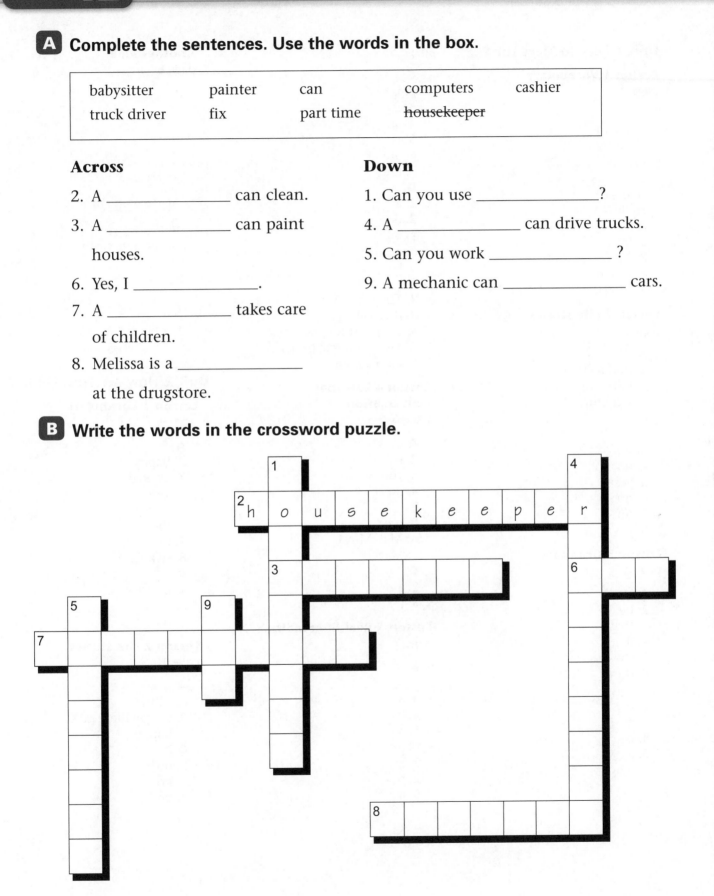

Unit 1 Nice to Meet You

Lesson 1 Vocabulary
page 2

A
open – 1
close – 2
say – 6
check – 5
sign – 3
circle – 4

B
2. Sign
3. Say
4. Circle
5. Check

Lesson 2 Life stories
page 3

A
2. middle name
3. last name
4. signature

B
2. no
3. yes
4. no
5. yes
6. no
7. no
8. yes

Lesson 3 Grammar
page 4

A
2. he
3. they
4. it
5. she
6. they

B
2. b
3. a
4. b
5. a

page 5

C
2. is
3. is
4. are
5. is
6. are
7. are

D
2. a
3. d
4. f
5. e
6. b

E
2. They are women.
3. It is a clock.
4. We are students.
5. My first name is Rosa.
6. I am a man.

Lesson 4 Everyday conversation
page 6

A
2. is
3. you
4. meet

B
B: me
A: Mal. M-A-L.
B: Mary

C
2. a
3. b

Lesson 5 Real-life reading
page 7

B
2. b
3. a
4. b
5. a
6. b
7. a
8. b
9. a

Another look
page 8

A

B
2. e
3. a
4. o
5. u

Unit 2 How Are You Feeling?

Lesson 1 Vocabulary
page 9

A
2. happy
3. excited
4. sad
5. hungry
6. thirsty
7. tired
8. sick

B
2. no
3. yes
4. no

Lesson 2 Life stories
page 10

A
2. China
3. Greenville, Texas
4. happy

B
2. no
3. no
4. no

Lesson 3 Grammar
page 11

A
2. b
3. b
4. a
5. b
6. a

B
2. is not
3. are not
4. is not
5. is
6. are

C
2. c
3. a

D
2. am not
3. are not
4. are not
5. is not
6. is not

page 12

E
2. She's from Haiti.
3. You're not thirsty.
4. I'm from Dallas, Texas.
5. They're not hungry.
6. We're fine.

F
2. He's not a teacher.
3. He's in Riverside.

G
2. I'm happy.
3. He's from Colorado.
4. We're not hungry.
5. It's not my book.
6. They're sick.

Lesson 4 Everyday conversation
page 13

A
2. feeling
3. I'm
4. sorry

B
2. c
3. a
4. e
5. b

Lesson 5 Real-life reading
page 14

B
2. yes
3. yes
4. no
5. no
6. no

C
2. Springfield
3. 31329
4. Luis Salas
5. Lee Street
6. 1242 Lee Street, Rincon, GA 31326

Another look
page 15

A
2. c
3. d
4. b

B
2. e
3. o
4. u
5. a

Unit 3 What time is it?

Lesson 1 Vocabulary
page 16

A
2. a
3. c
4. e
5. b
6. d

B
2. noon
3. afternoon
4. evening
5. night
6. midnight

Lesson 2 Life stories
page 17

A
2. clinic
3. store
4. library
5. school
6. English class
7. home

B
Morning: 10:30 a.m., 7:45 a.m.
Afternoon: 1:30 p.m., 2:15 p.m.

Lesson 3 Grammar
page 18

A
2. Are
3. Is
4. Are
5. Is

B
2. b
3. a
4. d

C
2. b
3. a
4. a
5. b
6. b

D
2. is
3. is
4. am
5. are
6. is

E
2. No, we're not.
3. No, I'm not.
4. No, it's not.
5. No, she's not.
6. No, he's not.

F
2. Is Susan sick?
3. Are the students in English class?
4. Are you at the library?
5. Is it 6:45?

Lesson 4 Everyday conversation
page 20

A
2. 10:00
3. library
4. is

B
2. c
3. a
4. e
5. b

Lesson 5 Real-life reading
page 21

B
2. no
3. yes
4. yes

Another look

page 22

A
ACROSS
1. home
4. train
5. noon
6. midnight
8. minutes
DOWN
2. evening
3. morning
7. time

B

Unit 4 What day is it?

Lesson 1 Vocabulary
page 23

A
2. Tuesday
3. Wednesday
4. Thursday
5. Friday
6. Saturday
7. Sunday
8. weekend
9. week

B
2. no
3. no
4. yes

Lesson 2 Life stories
page 24

A
2. June
3. July
4. month
5. August

B
Days of the week: Thursday, Sunday, Friday
Months: March, December, October

Lesson 3 Grammar
page 25

A
2. a
3. b
4. b
5. b
6. a

B
2. The party (*or* class party) is at 3:00.
3. The party (*or* birthday party) is on Saturday.
4. The party (*or* birthday party) is at 5:00.

C
2. When
3. What

D
2. b
3. a
4. e
5. f
6. c

E
2. My class is at Maple Adult School.
3. The birthday party is on Tuesday.
4. The party is at my house.
5. English class is on Thursday.
6. My birthday is in January.

Lesson 4 Everyday conversation
page 27

A
2. 9:00
3. Goodbye
4. Thursday

B
B: Wednesday
A: weekend
B: week

Lesson 5 Real-life reading
page 28

B
2. 9, 13
3. April 21
4. April 23
5. Thursdays

C
2. yes
3. no
4. no
5. no

6. yes

Another look
page 29

A

B
2. o
3. e
4. u
5. a

Unit 5 How much is it?

Lesson 1 Vocabulary
page 30

A
dime – 6
coins – 3
nickel – 5
quarter – 7
cents – 8
bills – 2
dollar – 1

B
2. c
3. d
4. a

Lesson 2 Life stories
page 31

A
2. pants
3. socks
4. shirt
5. expensive
6. cheap

B
2. no
3. yes
4. no

Lesson 3 Grammar
page 32

A
2. That
3. This
4. That

B
2. a
3. a
4. b

page 33

C
2. Those pants are $80.
3. Those pants are expensive.
4. These pizzas are $5.
5. These pizzas are cheap.
6. Those pizzas are $15.

D
2. f
3. d
4. a
5. b
6. e

E
2. These
3. Those
4. This
5. Those

Lesson 4 Everyday conversation
page 34

A
2. $36
3. much
4. It's
5. Thanks

B
2. $17, $17
3. $15, $15
4. $9.25, $9.25

Lesson 5 Real-life reading
page 35

B
2. a
3. b
4. b
5. a
6. b
7. a

Another look
page 36

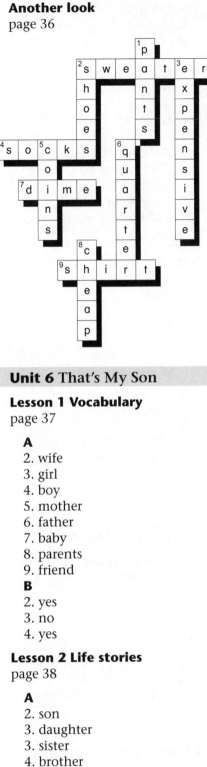

Unit 6 That's My Son

Lesson 1 Vocabulary
page 37

A
2. wife
3. girl
4. boy
5. mother
6. father
7. baby
8. parents
9. friend

B
2. yes
3. no
4. yes

Lesson 2 Life stories
page 38

A
2. son
3. daughter
3. sister
4. brother

B
2. yes
3. yes
4. no

Lesson 3 Grammar
page 39

A
2. her
3. her

4. their
5. his

B
2. b
3. a
4. b
5. a

page 40

C
2. live
3. lives

D
2. lives
3. live
4. live
5. live
6. live

E
2. Our parents live in Korea.
3. My daughter lives in Colorado.
4. His sister lives in North Carolina.
5. Their mother lives in New York.
6. Your son lives in Haiti.

Lesson 4 Everyday conversation
page 41

A
2. my
3. What's
4. name

B
3. 3

Lesson 5 Real-life reading
page 42

B
2. high
3. comes
4. good
5. homework

Another look
page 43

A
ACROSS
5. Mrs.
7. lives
8. wife
9. every day

DOWN
1. baby
3. single
4. friend
6. sister

B

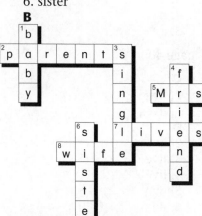

Unit 7 Do we need apples?

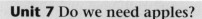

Lesson 1 Vocabulary
page 44

A
2. apples
3. grapes
4. oranges
5. cabbage
6. corn
7. broccoli
8. fruit
9. vegetables

B
2. bananas
3. apples
4. corn

Lesson 2 Life stories
page 45

A
2. beef
3. chicken
4. rice
5. vegetables

B
Fruit: oranges, bananas
Vegetable: corn, cabbage
Meat: lamb, chicken

Lesson 3 Grammar
page 46

A
2. don't
3. doesn't
4. don't

5. doesn't
6. doesn't

B
2. a
3. b
4. b
5. a
6. b

C
2. We don't like cabbage.
3. The teacher doesn't like fruit.
4. I don't like lamb.
5. The boy doesn't like bread.

page 47

D
2. does
3. do
4. do
5. does

E
2. b
3. e
4. c
5. a

F
2. The students need an English dictionary.
3. Ms. Reza needs oranges.
4. We don't live in Washington.
5. The children don't like eggs.
6. You don't like chicken.

Lesson 4 Everyday conversation
page 48

A
2. Paul: Here you go.
3. Fatima: Thanks.
4. Paul: You're welcome.

B
2. 2, 4, 4
3. 3, 6, 6
4. 2, 8, 8

Lesson 5 Real-life reading
page 49

B
2. yes
3. no
4. no
5. no
6. yes

C
2. oranges

3. chicken
4. 6
5. 1
6. 3

Another look
page 50

A

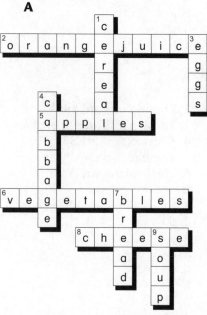

Unit 8 Take Two Tablets

Lesson 1 Vocabulary
page 51

A
2. ear
3. nose
4. head
5. hand
6. arm
7. stomach
8. leg
9. foot

B
2. no
3. yes

Lesson 2 Life stories
page 52

A
2. c
3. b
4. a
5. d
6. f

B

2. no
3. yes
4. no
5. yes
6. yes

Lesson 3 Grammar
page 53

A

2. You have a cough.
3. She has a headache.
4. He has an earache.
5. We have colds (or the flu).
6. They have stomachaches.

B

2. has
3. have
4. has
5. have
6. has

page 54

C

2. a
3. d
4. e
5. b

D

2. does
3. do
4. do

E

2. Do they have eggs?
3. Do you have a quarter?
4. Does he have a car?
5. Do we have paper?

F

2. A: Does; B: has
3. A: Do; B: have
4. A: Do; B: have
5. A. Do; B: have

Lesson 4 Everyday conversation
page 55

A

2. doctor
3. matter
4. flu
5. name
6. Rosita
7. 11:00
8. thank

B

B: Springfield
A: sick
B: stomachache
A: sorry
B: See, Saturday

Lesson 5 Real-life reading
page 56

B

2. b
3. a
4. a
5. b
6. b

Another look
page 57

A

2. o
3. i
4. e
5. u

B

2. b
3. c
4. e
5. d

Unit 9 What size?

Lesson 1 Vocabulary
page 58

A

Colors: purple, red, green
Clothes: socks, shirt, shoes

B

2. white
3. green
4. orange
5. blue
6. red
7. yellow
8. brown
9. black

Lesson 2 Life stories
page 59

A

2. cap
3. dress
4. jacket
5. boots
6. belt

B

2. no
3. yes
4. yes
5. no
6. no

Lesson 3 Grammar
page 60

A

2. are
3. is
4. are
5. am
6. are

B

2. She is wearing a coat.
3. She is wearing pants.
4. They are wearing T-shirts.
5. They are wearing shorts.
6. They are wearing caps.

C

2. b
3. a
4. a

page 61

D

2. Is
3. Is
4. Are
5. Are

E

2. b
3. a
4. a
5. a

F

2. Lila is sleeping.
3. He is wearing black shoes.
4. They are going to a party.

Lesson 4 Everyday conversation
page 62

A

2 Clerk: What size?
3 Eva: Medium
4 Clerk: Here's a medium.
5 Eva: Thanks.

B

2. $12.50
3. $35.00
4. $2.53

C

$53.03

Lesson 5 Real-life reading
page 63

B
2. a
3. b
4. b
5. b
6. a

C
2. cool
3. raining
4. cold

Another look
page 64

Unit 10 Where's the bank?

Lesson 1 Vocabulary
page 65

A
bank – 9
drugstore – 5
bookstore – 6
restaurant – 4
laundromat – 8
post office – 1
bus station – 7
park – 2

B
2. drugstore
3. bookstore
4. bank

Lesson 2 Life Stories
page 66

A
2. next to
3. across from
4. on the corner
5. between
6. restaurant

B
2. no
3. no
4. yes
5. no
6. yes

Lesson 3 Grammar
page 67

A
2. b
3. a
4. a
5. a

B
2. There are two restaurants.
3. There is a bank.
4. There are two houses.
5. There is a park.

page 68

C
2. Is
3. isn't
4. is
5. is

D
2. Is there an office on the corner?
3. Is there a park next to the bank?
4. Is there an elementary school nearby?

E
2. There is a bus station nearby.
3. No, there isn't.
4. There is a laundromat on Fifth Street.
5. There is a supermarket nearby.
6. There is a post office on the corner.

Lesson 4 Everyday conversation
page 69

A
2. Vinh: Yes, there is. It's between the bank and the bookstore.
3. Hector: Thank you.
4. Vinh: You're welcome.

B
2. 18
3. 25

Lesson 5 Real-life reading
page 70

B
2. fire station
3. (702) 555-5885
4. Third
5. court@springcity.us
6. 4545 Pine Street
7. dmv@springcity.us
8. First

Another look
page 71

A
1. a
3. d
4. c

B
2. a
3. e
4. u
5. i

Unit 11 This Is My Home

Lesson 1 Vocabulary
page 72

A
2. room
3. bed
4. dresser
5. furniture
6. stove
7. refrigerator
8. sofa
9. TV

B
2. no
3. yes
4. no

Lesson 2 Life stories
page 73

A
2. bedroom
3. bathroom
4. above
5. below
6. garage
7. on
8. in

B
Rooms: living room, kitchen
Furniture: sofa, stove

Lesson 3 Grammar
page 74

A
2. c
3. e
4. a
5. b

B
2. Mr. and Mrs. Lim's
3. Phu's
4. Kara's
5. Ingrid's

C
2. Lin's
3. Sara's
4. Galina's

page 75

D
2. b
3. a
4. a

E
[Note: Answers may appear in a different order.]
2. How many apples are there? One.
3. How many bananas are there? Two.
4. How many TVs are there? One.
5. How many chairs are there? Two.

F
2. Peng's living room has two sofas.
3. Orane's calendar is black and white.
4. Jenny and Olivia's books are expensive.

Lesson 4 Everyday conversation
page 76

A
2. there
3. rent
4. $1,000
5. many
6. Three

B
$2,200

Lesson 5 Real-life reading
page 77

B
2. b
3. a
4. b
5. a

Another look
page 78

Unit 12 Yes, I can!

Lesson 1 Vocabulary
page 79

A
cashier – 4
salesperson – 7
painter – 8
housekeeper – 3
hairdresser – 2
mechanic – 5
truck driver – 1
gardener – 9

B
2. yes
3. no
4. no

Lesson 2 Life stories
page 80

A
2. sell clothes
3. use computers
4. cut hair

B
Jobs: gardener, housekeeper, painter
Job skills: clean, take care of plants, paint houses

Lesson 3 Grammar
page 81

A
2. I can't fix the computer.
3. Dara can fix the computer.
4. Mateo can paint houses.
5. He can speak English.
6. He can't drive.

B
2. Marco, Min, and Alba can't use a computer.
3. Marco and Min can drive a car.
4. Min and Alba can't speak English.
5. Min can take care of plants/drive a car.

page 82

C
2. b
3. a
4. a
5. b

D
2. b
3. e
4. a
5. c

E
2. A: Can; B: can't
3. A: Can; B: can
4. A: Can; B: can
5. A: Can; B: can't

Lesson 4 Everyday conversation
page 83

A
2. Yes
3. evenings
4. can't

B
B: can
A: Can, clothes
B: can't
A: Can, car
B: can
A: Can, clean
B: can

Lesson 5 Real-life reading
page 84

B

2. b

3. b

4. a

5. b

6. a

Another look
page 85

A

ACROSS

3. painter

4. babysitter

7. cashier

8. can

DOWN

1. computers

4. truck driver

5. fix

9. part time

B

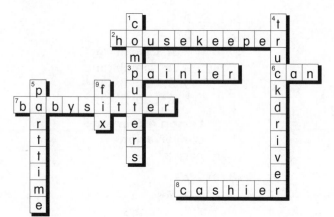

Step Forward
Language for Everyday Life

- **A standards-based, four-skills series emphasizing the language skills needed to be successful at home, in the community, and at work.**
- **Uniquely developed to meet the needs of both single-level and multilevel classrooms.**
- **Ideal partner to *The Basic Oxford Picture Dictionary* and *The Oxford Picture Dictionary*.**

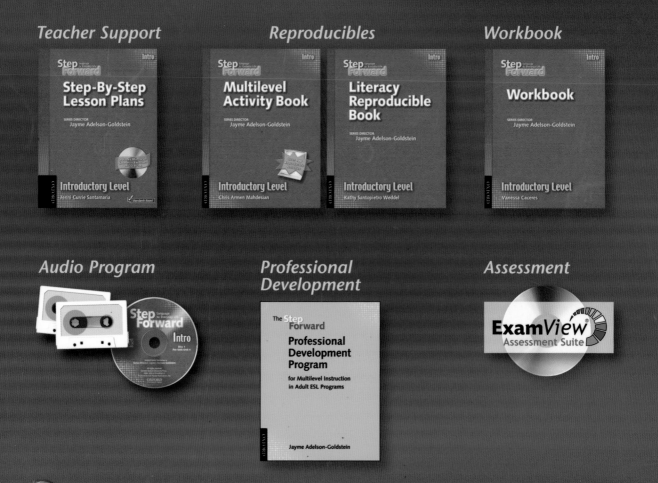

Teacher Support

Step-By-Step Lesson Plans
SERIES DIRECTOR
Jayme Adelson-Goldstein
Introductory Level
Jenni Currie Santamaria

Reproducibles

Multilevel Activity Book
SERIES DIRECTOR
Jayme Adelson-Goldstein
Introductory Level
Chris Armen Mahdesian

Literacy Reproducible Book
SERIES DIRECTOR
Jayme Adelson-Goldstein
Introductory Level
Kathy Santopietro Weddel

Workbook

Workbook
SERIES DIRECTOR
Jayme Adelson-Goldstein
Introductory Level
Vanessa Caceres

Audio Program

Professional Development

The Step Forward
Professional Development Program
for Multilevel Instruction in Adult ESL Programs
Jayme Adelson-Goldstein

Assessment

ExamView® Assessment Suite

About the Series Director

Jayme Adelson-Goldstein, co-author of *The Oxford Picture Dictionary* is an adult education ESL teacher, curriculum consultant, and certified teacher-trainer. She has given professional development workshops for adult education instructors throughout the United States on topics such as student-centered instruction, ESL techniques, and multilevel instruction.

To order **Oxford University Press** materials, please see

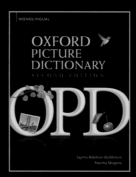

MONOLINGUAL
OXFORD PICTURE DICTIONARY
SECOND EDITION
OPD
Jayme Adelson-Goldstein
Norma Shapiro

OXFOR
UNIVERSITY PR.

www.oup.com

ISBN: 978 0 19 439844

9 780194 398442